Opposing Viewpoints®

PORNOGRAPHY

Opposing Viewpoints®

PORNOGRAPHY

Other Books of Related Interest

Opposing Viewpoints®

PORNOGRAPHY

Helen Cothran, *Book Editor*

Daniel Leone, *Publisher*
Bonnie Szumski, *Editorial Director*
Scott Barbour, *Managing Editor*

OPPOSING
VIEWPOINTS®
SERIES

Greenhaven Press, Inc., San Diego, California

Cover photo: Digital Vision

Library of Congress Cataloging-in-Publication Data

Pornography : opposing viewpoints / Helen Cothran, book editor.
    p. cm. — (Opposing viewpoints series)
    Includes bibliographical references and index.
    ISBN 0-7377-0761-5 (lib. bdg. : alk. paper) —
ISBN 0-7377-0760-7 (pbk. : alk. paper)
    1. Pornography. I. Cothran, Helen. II. Opposing viewpoints
series (Unnumbered)

HQ471 .P64619 2002
363.4'7—dc21
                                                    2001016036
                                                          CIP

Greenhaven Press, Inc., P.O. Box 289009
San Diego, CA 92198-9009

"Congress shall make no law. . .abridging the freedom of speech, or of the press."

First Amendment to the U.S. Constitution

The basic foundation of our democracy is the First Amendment guarantee of freedom of expression. The Opposing Viewpoints Series is dedicated to the concept of this basic freedom and the idea that it is more important to practice it than to enshrine it.

Contents

Why Consider Opposing Viewpoints?

"The only way in which a human being can make some approach to knowing the whole of a subject is by hearing what can be said about it by persons of every variety of opinion and studying all modes in which it can be looked at by every character of mind. No wise man ever acquired his wisdom in any mode but this."

John Stuart Mill

In our media-intensive culture it is not difficult to find differing opinions. Thousands of newspapers and magazines and dozens of radio and television talk shows resound with differing points of view. The difficulty lies in deciding which opinion to agree with and which "experts" seem the most credible. The more inundated we become with differing opinions and claims, the more essential it is to hone critical reading and thinking skills to evaluate these ideas. Opposing Viewpoints books address this problem directly by presenting stimulating debates that can be used to enhance and teach these skills. The varied opinions contained in each book examine many different aspects of a single issue. While examining these conveniently edited opposing views, readers can develop critical thinking skills such as the ability to compare and contrast authors' credibility, facts, argumentation styles, use of persuasive techniques, and other stylistic tools. In short, the Opposing Viewpoints Series is an ideal way to attain the higher-level thinking and reading skills so essential in a culture of diverse and contradictory opinions.

In addition to providing a tool for critical thinking, Opposing Viewpoints books challenge readers to question their own strongly held opinions and assumptions. Most people form their opinions on the basis of upbringing, peer pressure, and personal, cultural, or professional bias. By reading carefully balanced opposing views, readers must directly confront new ideas as well as the opinions of those with whom they disagree. This is not to simplistically argue that everyone who reads opposing views will—or should—change his or her opinion. Instead, the series enhances readers' understanding of their own views by encouraging confrontation with opposing ideas. Careful examination of others' views can lead to the readers' understanding of the logical inconsistencies in their own opinions, perspective on why they hold an opinion, and the consideration of the possibility that their opinion requires further evaluation.

Evaluating Other Opinions

To ensure that this type of examination occurs, Opposing Viewpoints books present all types of opinions. Prominent spokespeople on different sides of each issue as well as well-known professionals from many disciplines challenge the reader. An additional goal of the series is to provide a forum for other, less known, or even unpopular viewpoints. The opinion of an ordinary person who has had to make the decision to cut off life support from a terminally ill relative, for example, may be just as valuable and provide just as much insight as a medical ethicist's professional opinion. The editors have two additional purposes in including these less known views. One, the editors encourage readers to respect others' opinions—even when not enhanced by professional credibility. It is only by reading or listening to and objectively evaluating others' ideas that one can determine whether they are worthy of consideration. Two, the inclusion of such viewpoints encourages the important critical thinking skill of objectively evaluating an author's credentials and bias. This evaluation will illuminate an author's reasons for taking a particular stance on an issue and will aid in readers' evaluation of the author's ideas.

It is our hope that these books will give readers a deeper understanding of the issues debated and an appreciation of the complexity of even seemingly simple issues when good and honest people disagree. This awareness is particularly important in a democratic society such as ours in which people enter into public debate to determine the common good. Those with whom one disagrees should not be regarded as enemies but rather as people whose views deserve careful examination and may shed light on one's own.

Thomas Jefferson once said that "difference of opinion leads to inquiry, and inquiry to truth." Jefferson, a broadly educated man, argued that "if a nation expects to be ignorant and free . . . it expects what never was and never will be." As individuals and as a nation, it is imperative that we consider the opinions of others and examine them with skill and discernment. The Opposing Viewpoints Series is intended to help readers achieve this goal.

David L. Bender and Bruno Leone,
Founders

Greenhaven Press anthologies primarily consist of previously published material taken from a variety of sources, including periodicals, books, scholarly journals, newspapers, government documents, and position papers from private and public organizations. These original sources are often edited for length and to ensure their accessibility for a young adult audience. The anthology editors also change the original titles of these works in order to clearly present the main thesis of each viewpoint and to explicitly indicate the opinion presented in the viewpoint. These alterations are made in consideration of both the reading and comprehension levels of a young adult audience. Every effort is made to ensure that Greenhaven Press accurately reflects the original intent of the authors included in this anthology.

Introduction

"Two kinds of people in this world never quit: those who want to pass dirty pictures around, and those who want to stop them. It's an ancient conflict, one that's not likely ever to be resolved."

—*John Schwartz, staff writer for the* Washington Post

In 1908, archaeologist Josef Szombathy discovered a small naked figurine in the mud outside Willendorf, Austria. The "Venus of Willendorf"—as the ancient figurine was called— had pendulous breasts, exposed vulva, and large buttocks. More Venus figurines were discovered throughout Europe, and their overt sexuality led to heated conflict among archaeologists: Were the Venuses pornographic art, or were they ancient fertility goddesses celebrating women? Those studying the Venuses were influenced by contemporary attitudes about sexual imagery, and many were disturbed by the figurine's eroticism. As a result, the Venuses were kept out of beginning art books for nearly sixty years after their discovery, in spite of their historic and artistic importance. The sexual revolution in the 1960s and the feminist movement helped change attitudes about female sexuality, and eventually the Venuses were accepted by many—especially women—as symbols of Mother Earth.

Preoccupation with nudity and sex is by no means unique to ancient times, of course. Many contemporary magazines such as *Playboy*, for example, have enjoyed extended popularity and boast an international audience. Archaeologists centuries in the future might look upon their photographs of naked women much as modern archaeologists speculate about the Venuses, and ask whether they were meant to arouse, to celebrate sexuality, or to honor the fecundity of women.

It has always been difficult to define the difference between pornography, art, and erotica, and to measure the effects that any sexually explicit material has on society. As a result, pornography has long engendered both intense support and virulent opposition. Many people would be highly reluctant to place the Venus figurines and *Playboy* magazine in the same category, for example. The ancient artifacts are art, they might argue, while the "girlie" magazines clearly are not. Others might contend that photographs—even of naked women—are indeed art. Many commentators would assert that the purpose of *Playboy* images is clearly to arouse, while the purpose of the artifacts was more likely spiritual or celebratory.

"Pornography" has been a part of human experience since people first formed clay into human shapes. For centuries, the production of sexually explicit materials was rudimentary, as the ancient figurines illustrate. Eventually, with the invention of the printing press, however, sexually explicit material could be made and distributed more efficiently. In response, opponents applied an effective brake on its consumption. In the 1700s, the English editor Thomas Bowdler expurgated obscene passages from the works of Shakespeare. In the early 1900s, American social reformer Anthony Comstock convinced Congress to pass obscenity laws that allowed police to seize materials that discussed female sexuality and birth control.

By contrast, today magazines such as *Playboy* are routinely delivered to mailboxes across the United States. *Playboy*, first published in 1953, changed the way many people thought about nudity and sex. The magazine—because it featured naked women with girl-next-door looks, and included articles on politics and fashion—legitimated pornography. Men no longer hid their porn but purchased it openly.

Acceptance of *Playboy* and its ilk was not universal, however. When the women's movement gained momentum in the 1970s, many feminists attacked *Playboy* and similar magazines as damaging to women. Although these magazines were protected speech under the First Amendment, many feminists questioned that protection. Considered "soft-core" because they limited their content to depictions of naked women, these magazines were labeled pornography, not obscenity. Obscenity—"hard-core" images featuring sexual intercourse, bestiality, violence, and pedophilia—was still illegal because it was considered by the courts to be speech that was harmful to society. But many feminists believed that *Playboy* also constituted harmful speech because all pornog-

15

raphy denigrated women and therefore led to violence against them. However, U.S. courts have continued to uphold the distinction between pornography and obscenity.

Meanwhile, although print pornography was becoming more widely accepted, people still had to brave often-seedy X-rated movie houses if they wanted to see motion picture pornography. When home VCRs became widely available in the 1980s, however, people began to watch pornographic movies in the privacy of their own homes. So popular were such films that the pornography industry is credited with playing a large role in the rapid development of affordable VCRs.

In a similar manner, advances in computer technology in the 1990s radically changed how pornography was produced and consumed. Many of those involved in the pornography industry began to set up websites on the Internet that provided a variety of attractions, including photographs of people having sex, online catalogs of sex videos for sale, and—most recently—amateur video. Amateur videos are made by ordinary people who film themselves having sex, and then sell their "home movies" to sex sites.

Predictably, the proliferation of sexually explicit material on the Internet has led to renewed pressure to regulate pornography. The ease with which people—especially children—can now access sexually explicit material has intensified the debate about whether pornography should be illegal. Pro-sex feminists, adult sex industry workers, pornography consumers, and civil libertarians argue that censoring pornography would do more harm than good. Federal judge Sara Barker argues, for example, that "to deny free speech in order to engineer social change in the name of accomplishing a greater good for one sector of our society erodes the freedoms of all."

Although those opposed to censorship agree on the dangers of such limits on freedom, people in this camp often heatedly disagree about pornography's effects on society. Some contend that pornography helps people learn about their bodies and demystifies sex. As Kathleen Sullivan, Stanford University law professor puts it, "pornography is a charter of sexual revolution that is potentially liberating rather than confining to women." Others maintain that it leads to violence against women, child molestation, and the breakdown of the family. Ironically, those who favor censorship often cite these same effects of pornography in arguing their case. Catharine MacKinnon, law professor at Harvard University, claims that "pornography is the perfect preparation—motivator and instructional manual in one—for sexual atrocities [against women]."

The purpose of this anthology is to examine conflicting contemporary views on pornography and explore how technology may shape the production and consumption of pornography in the future. Academics, journalists, and activists debate how society should respond to pornography in the following chapters: Is Pornography Harmful? Should Pornography Be Censored? How Should Internet Pornography Be Regulated? What Should Be the Feminist Stance on Pornography? The debate over the Venus figurines, the popularity of *Playboy* magazine, and the emergence of Internet sex sites all suggest that the human preoccupation with pornography will continue well into the future.

CHAPTER 1

Is Pornography Harmful?

Chapter Preface

Waiting on Florida's death row to be executed, convicted serial killer Ted Bundy told an interviewer that violence-laced pornography had incited him to murder twelve-year-old Kimberly Leach and some thirty other young women.

People who believe that pornography is harmful point to criminals such as Ted Bundy as proof that pornography causes violence against women. In an interview with James Dobson of *Focus on the Family*, Bundy admitted that he saw pornography as "an indispensable link in the chain of behavior, the chain of events that led to the behavior, to the assaults, to the murders." Psychologist Edward Donnerstein contends that violent pornography causes ordinary men—not just sexual deviants—to become desensitized to rape. In a more general sense, many critics claim that pornography demeans people and damages morality.

Many people disagree that pornography is harmful, however. Defenders of sexually explicit material assert that pornography has never been proven to cause violence against women. They argue that violent criminals such as Ted Bundy are exceptions. Millions of men view pornography, they point out, and never commit a sex crime. In fact, pornography supporters claim that pornography can help relieve sexual tension in men and prevent violence. Others maintain that the consumption of pornography benefits women by freeing them from traditional beliefs about female sexuality. Some of these advocates contend that conservatives unfairly blame pornography for social ills because it challenges their traditional notions of femininity and sexuality. Nina Hartley, an actress who stars in adult films, contends that sexuality "is at the root of our essence as humans and that its perversion by religious fear has created the dire state of our existence today."

When Ted Bundy was executed in 1989 for the slaying of Kimberly Leach, people began to argue even more vociferously about how to gauge pornography's effects on consumers. The authors in the following chapter debate whether or not pornography harms women and degrades morality or whether it provides sexual release for men and helps women understand their own sexuality.

"*Historically, courts have recognized, and Congress has concluded, that pornography greatly harms individuals and society.*"

Pornography Harms Society

H. Robert Showers

In the following viewpoint, H. Robert Showers contends that pornography has a destructive impact on individuals and society. Showers argues that pornography debases the men who view it and leads to child molestation and violence against women. He maintains that obscenity and child pornography are not protected speech under the First Amendment and should be eradicated. H. Robert Showers is legal counsel to the National Coalition for the Protection of Children and Families, an organization that works to stop the harm caused by obscenity and child pornography.

As you read, consider the following questions:
1. Why were Barnes and Noble bookstores indicted in 1998, according to Showers?
2. According to the author, what is the legal definition of obscenity?
3. What percentage of pornography seized by customs was child pornography, according to Showers?

Reprinted from H. Robert Showers, "Myths and Misconceptions About Pornography: What You Don't Know Can Hurt You," 1998, by permission of the National Coalition for the Protection of Children and Families.

The horribly destructive impact of pornography on individuals and society has been the subject of much discourse, particularly since the U.S. Attorney General's Commission on Pornography released its findings in June of 1986 on the production, distribution, content and impact of hardcore and child pornography. The Meese Commission made 92 recommendations for federal, state and local governmental action and for citizen involvement. The recommendations included legislative action for obscenity and child pornography; involved executive branch and law enforcement activity to enhance investigative and prosecutorial activities; and recommended that the judiciary impose appropriate sentences.

After receiving the Commission's report, the Attorney General's office studied its recommendations and developed a seven-point plan of action. Every aspect of that plan went into effect. Congress adopted every recommendation for federal criminal law. A task force was formed within the U.S. Department of Justice, now called the Child Exploitation and Obscenity Section, to wage a full-time offensive against illegal pornography.

As a result of these efforts, indictments rose dramatically against distributors, mail order distribution of pornography decreased and prosecution of child pornographers increased.

These advances, though, have suffered in the last several years under Bill Clinton's administration beginning with a Justice Department attempt to re-define criteria for judging child obscenity. In addition, the Department has not aggressively pursued child obscenity violations.

However, in Alabama, state prosecutors are deftly targeting child obscenity. On February 18, 1998, Alabama Attorney General Bill Pryor announced the indictment of Barnes & Noble Booksellers on charges of selling child pornography in its stores. The books in question, *The Age of Innocence* by David Hamilton and *Radiant Identities* by Jock Sturges have caused concern nationwide because of their blatant, explicit use of children for sexual purposes.

Yet despite the state's efforts, another mounting threat to children state- and nationwide is the pornography available through computer online services. Much of the pornography business has now gone online because of easy access and the difficulty of tracing both users and distributors.

Unfortunately, attempts to regulate and outlaw pornography within a community are frequently criticized as censorship and a violation of the First Amendment right to free

Adult Entertainment Revenues

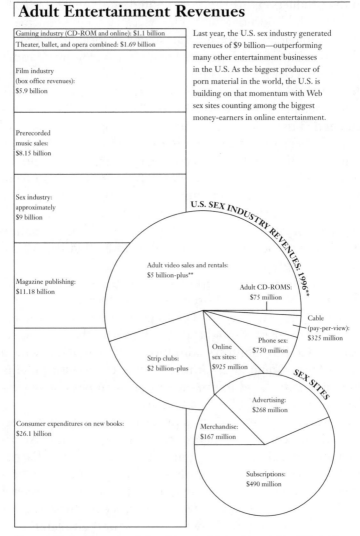

Gaming industry (CD-ROM and online): $1.1 billion

Theater, ballet, and opera combined: $1.69 billion

Film industry
(box office revenues):
$5.9 billion

Prerecorded
music sales:
$8.15 billion

Sex industry:
approximately
$9 billion

Magazine publishing:
$11.18 billion

Consumer expenditures on new books:
$26.1 billion

Last year, the U.S. sex industry generated revenues of $9 billion—outperforming many other entertainment businesses in the U.S. As the biggest producer of porn material in the world, the U.S. is building on that momentum with Web sex sites counting among the biggest money-earners in online entertainment.

U.S. SEX INDUSTRY REVENUES: 1996**

Adult video sales and rentals:
$5 billion-plus**

Adult CD-ROMS:
$75 million

Cable
(pay-per-view):
$325 million

Phone sex:
$750 million

Online
sex sites:
$925 million

Strip clubs:
$2 billion-plus

SEX SITES

Advertising:
$268 million

Merchandise:
$167 million

Subscriptions:
$490 million

*Sources: Motion Picture Association of America; National Association of Music Merchants; Magazine Publishers of America; Live Broadway; Opera America Dance USA.

**Note: Estimated figures provided by Adult Video News; *U.S. News & World Report;* Naughty Linx.

Frank Rose, *Wired,* December 1992.

speech. For example, the Telecommunications Act of 1996, signed into law on February 8, was intended to help fight pornographers and pedophiles who prey on children through the Internet.

The American Civil Liberties Union filed suit seeking to strike the entire section of the Telecommunications Act banning dissemination of pornographic materials to minors [the Communications Decency Act]. Unfortunately, the law was overturned by the U.S. Supreme Court in 1997, citing vagueness about several of the provisions. However, the bill was rewritten to pass constitutional muster, and as of the writing, has been reintroduced in a Senate committee. In addition, a bill has been introduced in the Senate which would require public libraries receiving federal funding for online access to install filtering software on at least one internet terminal. Public schools receiving subsidies would be required to install the filtering software on all terminals [neither bill has passed].

In contrast, on another front, in June 1998 the U.S. Supreme Court dismissed claims of pornography purveyors and supported the constitutionality of a federal law banning the sale or rental of pornographic material at military installations.

The Supreme Court has already ruled that obscenity is not protected by the First Amendment (Roth v. United States, 1957), yet there are several popular myths that keep the public from regarding illegal pornography, namely child pornography and obscenity, in its true light.

Myth No. 1: Obscenity Is in the Eye of the Beholder; It Cannot Be Defined

Obscenity is defined as the illegal form of pornography. Pornography is defined as "all sexually oriented material, primarily designed to arouse the reader or viewer." Commonly known as "hard-core" pornography, obscenity was given a clear legal definition in U.S. v. Roth and Miller v. California (1973), which states:

1. Whether patently offensive sexual conduct (ultimate sex acts, masturbation, sadomasochism, bestiality, excretory functions or lewd exhibitions of the genitals) is depicted substantially throughout the material such that;

23

2. It is directed toward an unhealthy, abnormal, morbid or shameful interest in sex; and
3. Taken as a whole, it lacks serious value.

Despite this straightforward language, individuals in favor of pornography often cite "vagueness" of definition as an excuse to escape prosecution. However, 29 major cities and one whole state (Utah) have completely eradicated hardcore pornography from their communities by enforcing these laws. Citizens of these areas have obviously found the existing definitions clear and the laws enforceable.

Myth No. 2: Obscenity and Child Pornography Are Protected Free Speech Under the First Amendment

Neither English common law nor the framers of the Constitution intended to protect obscene materials that exploit and degrade women and children. When the U.S. Supreme Court first examined the legal background of pornography in U.S. v. Roth, the Court concluded "there is sufficiently contemporaneous evidence with the Constitution to show that obscenity . . . was outside the protection intended for speech and press at the time during which the First Amendment was written." In fact, 13 of the 14 original states ratifying the Constitution and Bill of Rights in 1792 provided for prosecution of obscene libel, a less offensive form of expression. Repeatedly, the U.S. Supreme Court has emphatically confirmed that obscenity, child pornography and materials harmful to minors fall far below First Amendment protection.

Myth No. 3: Pornography Is a Victimless Crime

Historically, courts have recognized, and Congress has concluded, that pornography greatly harms individuals and society. In Paris Adult Theatre v. Slaton, the U.S. Supreme Court noted:

> The sum of experience affords an ample basis . . . to conclude that a sensitive, key relationship of human existency, centered to family life, community welfare, and the development of human personality, can be debased and distorted by crass, commercial exploitation of sex.

The most direct victims of illegal pornography are children. Out of 240,000 customs seizures over a five-year pe-

Masturbation and Pornography

In my experience as a sexual therapist, any individual who regularly masturbates to pornography is at risk of becoming, in time, a sexual addict, as well as conditioning himself into having a sexual deviancy and/or disturbing a bonded relationship with a spouse or girlfriend.

A frequent side effect is that it also dramatically reduces their capacity to love (e.g., it results in a marked dissociation of sex from friendship, affection, caring, and other normal healthy emotions and traits which help marital relationships). Their sexual side becomes in a sense dehumanized. Many of them develop an "alien ego state" (or dark side), whose core is antisocial lust devoid of most values.

In time, the "high" obtained from masturbating to pornography becomes more important than real life relationships. It has been commonly thought by health educators that masturbation has negligible consequences, other than reducing sexual tension. Moral objections aside, this may be generally true, but one exception would appear to be in the area of repeatedly masturbating to deviant pornographic imagery (either as memories in the mind or as explicit pornographic stimuli), which risks (via conditioning) the acquiring of sexual addictions and/or other sexual pathology.

It makes no difference if one is an eminent physician, attorney, minister, athlete, corporate executive college president, unskilled laborer, or an average 15-year-old boy. All can be conditioned into deviancy.

Victor B. Cline, "Pornography's Effects on Adults and Children," *World & I*, December 1992.

---

riod, over 70 percent were child pornography.

Even adult pornography takes minors as its victims. Of 1,400 child sexual molestation cases in Louisville, Kentucky, between July 1980 and February 1984, adult pornography was connected with each major case and child pornography with the majority of them. In addition, when children view or hear adult pornography, they not only receive sexual disinformation, but they model it. Just one example of this occurred in California where young children sexually molested a four-year-old girl after listening to "dial-a-porn" telephone messages promoting deviant sexual behavior and rape.

After children, women are obscenity's next victims, because pornography consumption is one of the most common profile characteristics of serial murderers and rapists. Obscenity takes other, more silent victims, too: marriages are torn apart; pornography-inflamed sexual abuse places families in crisis; and communities with pornographic outlets face devastating public health and safety concerns. In sum, as U.S. Supreme Court Chief Justice Warren emphasized, pornography jeopardizes the States' "right . . . to maintain a decent democratic society."

Federal and state leaders should take strong stands against the production and distribution of obscene material. In particular, they should strongly support cyberporn regulations as a significant step toward protecting America's children.

"Anti-porn groups, both feminist and religious, became obsessed with demonizing pornography."

Pornography Is Unfairly Blamed for Society's Ills

Lisa Palac

Lisa Palac was the founding editor of the cybersex magazine *Future Sex* and producer of the Virtual Reality CD series *Cyborgasm*. In the following viewpoint, Palac contends that because pornography challenges the sexual status quo, those who feel threatened by change blame it unfairly for social ills such as violence against women. She claims that snuff films—in which real women supposedly die at the hands of film crews—have come to symbolize what can happen if consumption of pornography is left unchecked. However, Palac maintains, no real snuff films exist, nor is pornography responsible for violence against women.

As you read, consider the following questions:
1. In Palac's opinion, why were witches persecuted from the fifteenth to eighteenth century?
2. What two famous feminists proposed anti-porn ordinances in several U.S. cities in the 1980s, according to the author?
3. Why are people fascinated with sexual monsters, according to Palac?

Nobody talks about *Snuff*[1] the movie these days. The tempest it generated has been forgotten. The assumption seems to be that everybody—especially feminists—knows what went down. Yet for the generations who came of age post-*Snuff*, and who feel the subject of pornography is important, most of them don't know. This film was a turning point in the feminist debates about pornography and sexuality. It galvanized the anti-porn feminist faction and led to the identification of pornography as the principal cause of women's oppression. The controversy reaffirmed porn's status as dangerous, low culture and supported the belief that bad images *cause* bad behavior, that pornography *causes* men to commit acts of sexual violence. It was a landslide moment in the history of sexual politics when anti-porn groups, both feminist and religious, became obsessed with demonizing pornography—the effects of which we are still confronting today.

The Power of Myth

While most people ask me about snuff films out of simple curiosity, a few wield the question like a weapon and they're looking for a fight. Go ahead, Little Miss Porn Cheerleader, let's hear you defend snuff films! Look, if someone presented me with a genuine snuff film there'd be nothing to defend. I would be horrified and sickened. But no one ever has and no one ever will because snuff films, as some kind of readily available, black-market commercial enterprise, don't exist. They're an urban myth.

Don't underestimate the power of myth, though. Myths link us together socially; they influence our moral choices, our political choices; they showcase human nature, bright and dark. They give us reason to believe, which is why the myth of snuff films has survived for so long, despite all the evidence to the contrary. We *want* to believe in snuff films because we have a collective need to believe in sexual monsters.

Throughout history, monsters have reflected our cultural anxieties and fears about sex. Jews, blacks, women,

---

1. *Snuff*—released in 1976—is a film which concludes with footage of the director of the film making sexual advances toward a female production assistant and then hacking her to pieces.

homosexuals—they've all played the demon. The monster, the Other, is born out of social crisis, a threat to the status quo. Belief in monsters unites us against a common enemy, reinforces the rules of sexual conduct, and allows us to justify some of our most extreme actions.

Pornography Is Powerful

Pornography is not ugly; our society's attitudes about sex are ugly. Pornography does not degrade the people in it; our society degrades people for desiring sex. Pornography is not shameful to enjoy; our society says we do not deserve the exquisite pleasure and joy that come from "coming". Pornography is powerful because it dares. Dares to shamelessly expose that which has been kept hidden, dares to give form to nameless desires. Shows life after the sharing of pleasure; shows men and women as equal sexual partners.

Nina Hartley, "Pornography at the Millennium," *Gauntlet*, 1997.

Take witches, for example. They fit the profile of a sexual monster to a T. From the fifteenth to the eighteenth century, thousands of European women were tortured and then burned alive for allegedly practicing witchcraft. The fear? Female sexuality. The monstrous allegation was that witches fornicated with the devil, thereby bringing evil into the world. In reality, they were healers, herbalists and midwives who revered the power of nature. And more often than not, a witch was simply whatever poor soul the mob chose to persecute. Witches gave everyone, Catholic and Protestant alike, a scapegoat for the evils of the day—poverty, disease, violence, mental illness, sexual desire, bad crops, bad luck. Plus, the threat of being marked as a witch kept everyone in line. Even the slightest display of nonconformity, sexual or otherwise, could mean a trip to the fire. Ultimately, the monster justified the massacre.

Protecting the Sexual Status Quo

In much the same way, snuff films meet the requirements of a sexual monster. A belief in snuff films goes hand in hand with the belief that pornography is evil, and that the sexual impulse itself is basically evil and needs to be controlled. Snuff films are a constant reminder of just how bad things can get if left unchecked: women getting fucked up and chopped up, men degenerating into sperm-spurting killing machines. The snuff film panic came at a time when the sexual status quo was being challenged from every cultural corner. Pornography had become chic, even attaining a level of respectability among the middle class. By 1973, the X-rated film *Deep Throat* was playing at theaters around the country, and images of explicit sex were no longer "obscene" in and of themselves; a work now had to be proven to lack serious literary, artistic, political or scientific value. So what new bold strategy could be used to tighten up those loose morals? Linking pornography with murder. Snuff films united two groups who would never have been seen in the same room together—right-wing Christians and radical feminists. The monster gave us a new reason to quash our erotic impulses—snuff or be snuffed—and justified attacks on the First Amendment. By 1985, the Meese Commission recommended greater restrictions of sexually explicit material based on the unconfirmed theory that pornography causes harm. Beginning in the mid-1980s and continuing well into the 1990s, writer Andrea Dworkin and attorney Catharine MacKinnon proposed anti-porn ordinances in Minneapolis, Indianapolis and Cambridge, Massachusetts, that would allow women to sue for damages for the harm caused by pornography. All three were ultimately voted down, but were a big success at stirring up fear. Censorship continues to be promoted as a necessary defense against the monsters who lurk somewhere out there.

The Allure of Sexual Monsters

But even for those of us who don't believe in the existence of devils or snuff films, there's no denying a universal fascination with sexual monsters. The success of horrifying movies, the stamina of gross-out urban legends, even the gruesome details of monstrous true crimes printed in the daily paper—they're all testaments to the fact that we're simultaneously attracted and repelled by the forbidden. As much as they frighten us, monsters appeal to us because they reflect our own desires to cross the lines we've drawn, to poke around in the darkest parts of our psyche, to know the Other side of ourselves. At the same time, we don't want to get too close. Monsters hand us a convenient yardstick to measure the distance between Us and Them (which is often frighteningly small) so we can feel secure, "normal" and even superior about our own sexual tastes—I'm not a monster, you are!

I also think sexual monsters and the fear they bring are an antidote to erotic boredom. We scare ourselves on purpose with all sorts of stories because feeling frightened makes us feel alive, utterly conscious of our own existence. Sex will always be exciting as long as there are lines to cross, monsters to confront and questions about just how close we are to the bottom of that slippery slope.

"The number one source of pornography currently, and in epidemic proportions, is the Internet."

Internet Pornography Is a Serious Problem

Mark Laaser

Mark Laaser is a recovering sex addict and executive director and cofounder of the Christian Alliance for Sexual Recovery. In the following viewpoint, Laaser argues that the Internet is now a primary source of pornography because it offers accessibility, affordability, and anonymity to consumers. He maintains that children can develop deviant sexual behavior from viewing Internet pornography and can be targeted by Internet pedophiles. Internet pornography can also lead to sexual addiction and unacceptable sexual behavior in adults, he contends.

As you read, consider the following questions:
1. How does Laaser support his contention that sex can become an addiction?
2. According to the author, how do some Internet pedophiles lure children into having encounters with them?
3. What is the fourth "A" that Laaser would add to Al Cooper's "Triple A Engine" concept?

Reprinted from Mark Laaser's testimony before the U.S. House of Representatives Committee on Commerce, Subcommittee on Telecommunications, Trade, and Consumer Protection, May 23, 2000.

Various research studies have demonstrated the escalating usage of sexually oriented sites on the Internet. In a 1998 study of hundreds of on-line users, Dr. Al Cooper found that 15% had accessed one of the top five sex web sites. A follow-up study in 1999 reported that 31% of on-line users visited web sites dedicated to pornography. In the most recent study, the Sexual Recovery Institute of Los Angeles conducted a research survey and found that 25 million Americans visit cyber-sex sites every week and that 60% of all web site visits are sexual in nature. It is estimated that by the year 2001, 95 million Americans will have access to the Internet.

The Prevalence of Internet Porn

In a 2000 issue of the journal *Sexual Addiction and Compulsivity* several authors contend that accessing sexually oriented web sites is not confined to the home but is a primary problem at work. One study by a leading Fortune 500 company found that 62% of male computer time was spent in cyber-sex sites. A friend of mine, who is a vice-president of one of our large Twin Cities based companies, recently had to fire 20 top level executives because of uncontrolled pornography usage on company owned computers.

It is commonly accepted by all researchers that sexually oriented web sites are a tremendous growth industry around the world. Hundreds of new ones are added every week. Entering even remotely sexually related words into any search engine will result in thousands of sexually based web site possibilities. . . .

While there has been some success in regulating web sites devoted to child pornography, most of this kind of pornography is trafficked through bulletin board systems with "picture files" that can be hidden in a variety of ways, and with Usenet News groups. These last use binary groups, digitized photographs, which can be transformed, in a variety of ways. This is not to mention the transmission of e-mails with photo attachments. While the most common depictions are of child nudity, children in erotic poses, and depictions of children in sexual activity, there is an incredible amount of depictions of rape, bondage, S&M, and adult-child intercourse.

Various Forms of Damage

Specialists in the field of sexuality can be divided about sexual material available on the Internet. Some even suggest that it has educational value, decreases some unhealthy inhibitions, and is an otherwise unavailable social outlet. Few would disagree, however, that certain forms of pornography, as just described above, are universally damaging.

Of chief concern should be possible damage to children. There can be little doubt for any of us parents that our children are more computer literate than we are. Even a five-year-old might have the computer skills to access any form of web site. Some have even suggested, as a result, that the average age a child first sees pornography has decreased from age 11 to age 5. We can't discount the other forms of pornography that are more readily available today than when I first saw pornography in 1961.

According to the book *Protecting Your Child in Cyberspace* by Steve Kavanagh, a licensed mental health professional, "There are many studies that suggest that exposure to pornography can make kids act out sexually against other children. . . . It seems clear that viewing deviant sexual behavior on the internet can cause a child to develop sexual deviance, which can shape sexual preferences that carry over into adulthood." In computer terms, a child's brain can be programmed neuro-anatomically for various forms of sexual orientation. While the brain can't manufacture new brain cells it continually manufactures connections between them.

Dr. John Money of Johns Hopkins University first described the theory that the brain is most critically programmed sexually during early childhood in his 1986 book *Lovemaps*. Dr. Money's groundbreaking work suggests that most forms of sexual deviance can be traced to experiences in childhood. Simply exposing a child to images of deviant sexual activity can have a profound effect. My own personal experience, and the experience of over a thousand clients would confirm this theory. I would emphasize that it is not just hard-core pornography that can have this effect. Many psychologists, such as Dr. Judith Riesman, argue that even the so-called "softer" forms, such as in popular magazines, can be just as damaging.

Cyberporn Addiction

Theories of sexual addiction and compulsivity are controversial in the clinical community. There is no doubt that the majority of on-line Internet users don't become addicted to the pornography that can be found there. There is also no doubt in my mind that many do. Some researchers are even starting to suggest that some who might not otherwise have become addicted to sex, are now doing so because of the Internet.

One of the stumbling blocks in the clinical debate about whether sex can be an addiction centers on the concept of chemical "tolerance." Many in the medical community feel that for substance or activity to be addictive it must create a chemical tolerance. Alcoholics know, for example, that over the lifetime of their addiction, they must consume more and more alcohol to achieve the same effect. New research, such as by Drs. Harvey Milkman and Stan Sunderwirth, has demonstrated that sexual fantasy and activity, because of naturally produced brain chemicals, has the ability to create brain tolerance to sex.

I have treated over a thousand male and female sex addicts. Almost all of them began with pornography. The number

Horsey. Reprinted with permission from North America Syndicate.

one source of pornography currently, and in epidemic proportions, is the Internet. It used to be that only men accessed sexually oriented web sites. Sadly, we are beginning to see an increase in the number of women who are addicted to pornography of all kinds, but mostly on the Internet.

The consequences of Internet pornography can be catastrophic. All of us who work in the field of sexual addiction have seen a marked increase in Internet addiction in the last year. Typically, our cases involve people who have lost jobs, vocations, and marriages due to Internet addiction. In a study of 91 women whose husbands were so addicted, for example, Jennifer Schneider, M.D. found that all felt hurt, betrayed, and rejected. All of these women felt unfavorably compared. 68% reported that their partner had become disinterested in sex with them. 22.3% attributed their divorce from these partners as due to the Internet.

As an addiction, Internet pornography can escalate. It may lead to other forms of sexual acting out. For some with accompanying personal pathologies, it may lead to sexual offenses. The physical and legal consequences to the addict and to others are obvious.

Chat Room Predators

Finally, we should be aware of the dangers of Internet chat rooms as a place where sexuality can be problematic. We are aware that sexual predators can be present in chat rooms disguised in a variety of ways. Pedophiles may even send pornographic pictures to prospective child victims as a way of "softening" them up to eventual encounters. This has been a known form of pedophilic ritual for years. We have all warned our children against talking to strangers, but the Internet makes healthy decisions in this regard less likely. A number of well-known cases in which children and teenagers have been recruited for eventual sexual activity should warn us of the dangers of chat rooms.

Adults, also, may get caught up in chat rooms. I have a client whose husband gave her a computer for Christmas. She says that she doesn't remember the month of January. She became addicted to the "romance" of on-line chat. Researchers and experts in the field of romance addiction, such as Pat Carnes, Ph.D. have clearly described that romance creates neurochemicals such as phenylethylamine (PEA) which would explain the addictive reaction of my client. My client's romance addiction escalated and she wound up actually meeting four of the men in person and developing a sexually transmitted disease as a result. I have had a number of clients who would fit this same profile.

On-line pornography and chat rooms appeal to those who are isolated, lonely and bored. When other emotional and neuro-chemical vulnerabilities are present, addictions can be the result.

The Uniqueness of the Internet

One of the reasons that the Internet is so dangerous is because of its certain uniqueness. Al Cooper, Ph.D. was the first to suggest the concept of the "Triple A Engine" of the Internet. He says that its uniqueness is that it is Accessible, Affordable, and Anonymous.

When I saw my first pornographic magazine, I had to be a detective to find what drug stores kept in some hidden cabinet. As an adult I had to go to many fairly sordid places to find what I was looking for. The point is both as an adolescent and as an adult I had to go looking. Today, the Internet has made it completely accessible to the youngest of users. There are forms of pornography available today that weren't available even in the most perverse of locations just five years ago. Every year we see a rise in the kinds of material that are easily available. Many communities, such as my own in Minneapolis, are facing the problem of the easy accessibility of pornography using computers in public schools and libraries. We are a free speech society. Recently, even the voters of a conservative city like Holland, Michigan, rejected putting filtering devices on public library computers.

Internet pornography is affordable. We know that many people who may have paid for something originally can transmit it to others for free. We also know that many sexually oriented web sites offer free pictures as an enticement to log in with a credit card. Such free enticements led one of my clients to become addicted to sex on the Internet. He eventually spent $85,000 in the month of February. If there are people who might otherwise restrict their use of pornography, or various more expensive forms of it, because of money, there is enough free material available to keep them going. The majority of my clients who are addicted to Internet pornography don't pay for it.

Internet Pedophiles

Internet pedophiles appear to have an avaricious appetite for pornography. Many of them have collected thousands of images, but they still risk trawling the semipublic channels seeking new material. The pornography traded on the Internet is done without charge so the only premium is on the "new" material. Asian children appear in large numbers. The male, white, and mainly middle-aged abusers are almost always hidden in the pictures with only their naked torsos or hands appearing. Among the most frightening pictures available across pedophile channels is a series that shows a girl of about nine or 10 being subjected to abuse involving bondage.

Jim Cusack, "The Murky World of Internet Porn," *World Press Review*, November 1996.

Several psychologists, such as Dr. Mark Schwartz, director of the Masters and Johnson Institute, have said that the anonymous nature of the Internet makes many more people vulnerable to it. He says that some who might not become compulsively involved in deviant sexual activities because of having to go to "dangerous" places and risking exposure, are now getting involved in the obscurity and "safety" of their homes. What this means is that more and more people are becoming more and more involved in sexually deviant forms of acting out. It used to be that "normal" people might have an aversion to going to places that catered to sexual deviance, such as S&M bars. Now through on-line pornography, chat, and exchange, it is much easier to become involved in these activities.

Accidental Exposure

To the "Triple A Engine" I would add a fourth "A," accidental. Those who have sought to protect the free speech rights of pornographers have long claimed that it is an individual's free choice to view pornography. On the Internet, however, pornography may come looking for you. All of us are familiar with the unsolicited e-mails that advertise sexually oriented web sites. That is one thing. The greater danger for those who otherwise seek to use the World Wide Web for constructive purpose is that they will accidentally be exposed to sexually oriented sites.

Recently, for example, parents that I know told me the story of how their 8-year-old daughter was researching the fairy tale Cinderella on the web. She entered Cinderella in the search engine of her on-line service provider. She was given a number of options. One of them included the title, "See Cinderella for Yourself." This little girl of course wanted to see Cinderella, so she clicked in. She was immediately confronted with the picture of a nude female using an artificial penis to stimulate herself. I would consider this to be a form of sexual assault.

Robert Freeman-Longo, a well-known sexologist and researcher, conducted a recent study using AOL, the largest on-line service provider. He entered the words "parental control" into the search engine. 12,508 sites came up including a wide variety of sexually oriented ones. Can there be any doubt that even if you are looking for certain types of materials, they may accidentally come to you? Some might even question whether or not some of this is accidental. Estimates are that 85% of the production of pornography in this country is controlled by organized crime. Do we doubt that this faction of our culture would be aggressive in "purveying" their product?

As a recovering sex addict, I am personally offended by the aggressive and unique nature of Internet pornography. If I were an alcoholic, there would be no one bringing free alcoholic beverages to my door. Yet, in my work I have a professional need to be on-line frequently. I am assaulted daily by sexual opportunities that I have not invited into my life or pursued.

> *"The issue of pornography on the Internet is a moral panic—an issue perpetuated by a sensationalistic style of reporting and misleading content in newspaper and magazine articles."*

The Problem of Internet Pornography Is Exaggerated

Julia Wilkins

Julia Wilkins has a master's degree in social policy from the University of Bristol, England. In the following viewpoint, she contends that articles in *Time* and *Newsweek* magazines have fueled a moral panic over Internet pornography. According to Wilkins, a moral panic over perceived threats to society is created when the media exaggerate, repeat inaccurate information, and use misleading pictures and sensationalized titles when reporting on the issue. Wilkins claims that pornography on the Internet is not as widespread or accessible as the media make it out to be.

As you read, consider the following questions:

1. What were the flaws in Marty Rimm's report, according to Wilkins?
2. According to the author, what other methods are there for protecting children from Internet pornography aside from regulation?
3. Why doesn't the media always tell the truth, according to Stanley Cohen?

Excerpted from Julia Wilkins, "Protecting Our Children from Internet Smut: Moral Duty or Moral Panic?" *The Humanist*, September/October 1997. Reprinted by permission of the author.

The term moral panic is one of the more useful concepts to have emerged from sociology in recent years. A moral panic is characterized by a wave of public concern, anxiety, and fervor about something, usually perceived as a threat to society. The distinguishing factors are a level of interest totally out of proportion to the real importance of the subject, some individuals building personal careers from the pursuit and magnification of the issue, and the replacement of reasoned debate with witchhunts and hysteria.

Creating Moral Panic

Moral panics of recent memory include the Joseph McCarthy anti-communist witchhunts of the 1950s and the satanic ritual abuse allegations of the 1980s. And, more recently, we have witnessed a full-blown moral panic about pornography on the Internet. Sparked by the July 3, 1995, *Time* cover article, "On a Screen Near You: Cyberporn," this moral panic has been perpetuated and intensified by a raft of subsequent media reports. As a result, there is now a widely held belief that pornography is easily accessible to all children using the Internet. This was also the judgment of Congress, which, proclaiming to be "protecting the children," voted overwhelmingly in 1996 for legislation to make it a criminal offense to send "indecent" material over the Internet into people's computers.[1]

The original *Time* article was based on its exclusive access to Marty Rimm's Georgetown University Law Journal paper, "Marketing Pornography on the Information Superhighway." Although published, the article had not received peer review and was based on an undergraduate research project concerning descriptions of images on adult bulletin board systems in the United States. Using the information in this paper, *Time* discussed the type of pornography available online, such as "pedophilia (nude pictures of children), hebephelia (youths) and . . . images of bondage, sadomasochism, urination, defecation, and sex acts with a barnyard full of animals." The article proposed that pornography of this nature is readily available to anyone who is even remotely computer literate

1. This law—called the Communications Decency Act (CDA)—was overturned in 1997.

and raised the stakes by offering quotes from worried parents who feared for their children's safety. It also presented the possibility that pornographic material could be mailed to children without their parents' knowledge. *Time's* example was of a ten-year-old boy who supposedly received pornographic images in his e-mail showing "10 thumbnail size pictures showing couples engaged in various acts of sodomy, heterosexual intercourse and lesbian sex." Naturally, the boy's mother was shocked and concerned, saying, "Children should not be subject to these images." *Time* also quoted another mother who said that she wanted her children to benefit from the vast amount of knowledge available on the Internet but was inclined not to allow access, fearing that her children could be "bombarded with X-rated pornography and [she] would know nothing about it."

From the outset, Rimm's report generated a lot of excitement—not only because it was reportedly the first published study of online pornography but also because of the secrecy involved in the research and publication of the article. In fact, the *New York Times* reported on July 24, 1995, that Marty Rimm was being investigated by his university, Carnegie Mellon, for unethical research and, as a result, would not be giving testimony to a Senate hearing on Internet pornography. Two experts from *Time* reportedly discovered serious flaws in Rimm's study involving gross misrepresentation and erroneous methodology. His work was soon deemed flawed and inaccurate, and *Time* recanted in public. With Rimm's claims now apologetically retracted, his original suggestion that 83.5 percent of Internet graphics are pornographic was quietly withdrawn in favor of a figure less than 1 percent.

Time admitted that grievous errors had slipped past their editorial staff, as their normally thorough research succumbed to a combination of deadline pressure and exclusivity agreements that barred them from showing the unpublished study to possible critics. . . .

The July 7, 1997, *Newsweek*, picking up the frenzy where *Time* left off, reported the 1997 Supreme Court decision [to overturn the Communications Decency Act—which would have made it illegal to transmit obscene material over the Internet] in a provocatively illustrated article featuring a color photo of a woman licking her lips and a warning message taken from the website of the House of Sin. Entitled "On the Net, Anything Goes," the opening words by Steven Levy read, "Born of a hysteria triggered by a genuine problem—the ease with which wired-up teenagers can get hold of nasty pictures on the Internet—the Communications Decency Act (CDA) was never really destined to be a companion piece to the Bill of Rights." At the announcement of the Court's decision, anti-porn protesters were on the street outside brandishing signs which read, "Child Molesters Are Looking for Victims on the Internet."

Online Recreation, Not Pathology

People have rather innocent, if extensive, appetites for sexual stimulation and information. What they want [from Internet pornography and online sex] is recreation rather than pathological outlets, amusement rather than a chance to prey on young innocents. What people tend to give each other through online sexual contact is companionship and support much more than manipulation and abuse.

David Steinberg, "Cyber Access: Power to the People," *Gauntlet*, 1998.

Meanwhile, government talk has shifted to the development of a universal Internet rating system and widespread hardware and software filtering. Referring to the latter, White House Senior Adviser Rahm Emanuel declared, "We're going to get the V-chip [a device that blocks television programs based upon their ratings] for the Internet. Same goal, different means."

But it is important to bear in mind that children are still a minority of Internet users. A contract with an Internet service provider typically needs to be paid for by credit card or direct debit, therefore requiring the intervention of an adult. Children are also unlikely to be able to view any kind of porn online without a credit card.

In addition to this, there have been a variety of measures developed to protect children on the Internet. The National Center for Missing and Exploited Children has outlined protective guidelines for parents and children in its pamphlet, Child Safety on the Information Superhighway. A number of companies now sell Internet newsfeeds and web proxy accesses that are vetted in accordance with a list of forbidden topics. And, of course, there remain those blunt software instruments that block access to sexually oriented sites by looking for keywords such as sex, erotic, and X-rated. But one of the easiest solutions is to keep the family computer in a well-traveled space, like a living room, so that parents can monitor what their children download.

Fact or Media Fiction?

In her 1995 *Computer-Mediated Communications* magazine article, "Journey to the Centre of Cybersmut," Lisa Schmeiser discusses her research into online pornography. After an exhaustive search, she was unable to find any pornography, apart from the occasional commercial site (requiring a credit card for access), and concluded that one would have to undertake extensive searching to find quantities of explicit pornography. She suggested that, if children were accessing pornography online, they would not have been doing it by accident. Schmeiser writes: "There will be children who circumvent passwords, Surfwatch software [which blocks sites containing keywords such as sex], and seemingly innocuous links to find the 'adult' material. But these are the same kids who would visit every convenience store in a five-mile radius to find the one stocking *Playboy*." Her argument is simply that, while there is a certain amount of pornography online, it is not freely and readily available. Contrary to what the media often report, pornography is not that easy to find.

There is pornography in cyberspace (including images, pictures, movies, sounds, and sex discussions) and several ways of receiving pornographic material on the Internet (such as through private bulletin board systems, the World Wide Web, newsgroups, and e-mail). However, many sites just contain reproduced images from hardcore magazines and videos available from other outlets, and registration fee restrictions make them inaccessible to children. And for the more contentious issue of pedophilia, a recent investigation by the *Guardian* newspaper in Britain revealed that the majority of pedophilic images distributed on the Internet are simply electronic reproductions of the small output of legitimate pedophile magazines, such as *Lolita*, published in the 1970s.

Clearly the issue of pornography on the Internet is a moral panic—an issue perpetuated by a sensationalistic style of reporting and misleading content in newspaper and magazine articles. And probably the text from which to base any examination of the possible link between media reporting and moral panics is Stanley Cohen's 1972 book, *Folk Devils and Moral Panic*, in which he proposes that the mass media are ultimately responsible for the creation of such panics. Cohen describes a moral panic as occurring when "a condition, episode, person or group of persons emerges to become a threat to societal values and interests; . . . the moral barricades are manned by editors . . . politicians and other 'right thinking' people." He feels that, while problematical elements of society can pose a threat to others, this threat is realistically far less than the perceived image generated by mass media reporting.

Cohen describes how the news we read is not necessarily the truth; editors have papers to sell, targets to meet, and competition from other publishers. It is in their interest to make the story "a good read"—the sensationalist approach sells newspapers. The average person is likely to be drawn in with the promise of scandal and intrigue. This can be seen in the reporting of the *National Enquirer* and *People*, with their splashy pictures and sensationalistic headlines, helping them become two of the largest circulation magazines in the United States.

Cohen discusses the "inventory" as the set of criteria inherent in any reporting that may be deemed as fueling a moral panic. This inventory consists of the following:

Exaggeration in Reporting

Facts are often overblown to give the story a greater edge. Figures that are not necessarily incorrect but have been quoted out of context, or have been used incorrectly to shock, are two forms of this exaggeration.

Looking back at the original *Time* cover article, "On a Screen Near You: Cyberporn," this type of exaggeration is apparent. Headlines such as "The Carnegie Mellon researchers found 917,410 sexually explicit pictures, short stories and film clips online" make the reader think that there really is a problem with the quantity of pornography in cyberspace. It takes the reader a great deal of further exploration to find out how this figure was calculated. Also, standing alone and out of context, the oftquoted figure that 83.5 percent of images found on Usenet Newsgroups are pornographic could be seen as cause for concern. However, if one looks at the math associated with this figure, one would find that this is a sampled percentage with a research leaning toward known areas of pornography.

The Repetition of Fallacies

This occurs when a writer reports information that seems perfectly believable to the general public, even though those who know the subject are aware it is wildly incorrect. In the case of pornography, the common fallacy is that the Internet is awash with nothing but pornography and that all you need to obtain it is a computer and a modem. Such misinformation is integral to the fueling of moral panics.

Take, for example, the October 18, 1995, *Scotland on Sunday*, which reports that, to obtain pornographic material, "all you need is a personal computer, a phone line with a modem attached and a connection via a specialist provider to the Internet." What the article fails to mention is that the majority of pornography is found on specific Usenet sites not readily available from the major Internet providers, such as America Online and Compuserve. It also fails to mention that this pornography needs to be downloaded and converted into a viewable form, which requires certain skills and can take considerable time.

Misleading Pictures and Snappy Titles

Media representation often exaggerates a story through provocative titles and flashy pictorials—all in the name of drawing in the reader. The titles set the tone for the rest of the article; the headline is the most noticeable and important part of any news item, attracting the reader's initial attention. The recent *Newsweek* article is a perfect example. Even if the headline has little relevance to the article, it sways the reader's perception of the topic. The symbolization of images further increases the impact of the story. *Time*'s own images in its original coverage—showing a shocked little boy on the cover and, inside, a naked man hunched over a computer monitor—added to the article's ability to shock and to draw the reader into the story.

Through sensationalized reporting, certain forms of behavior become classified as deviant. Specifically, those who put pornography online or those who download it are seen as being deviant in nature. This style of reporting benefits the publication or broadcast by giving it the aura of "moral guardian" to the rest of society. It also increases revenue.

In exposing deviant behavior, newspapers and magazines have the ability to push for reform. So, by classifying a subject and its relevant activities as deviant, they can stand as crusaders for moral decency, championing the cause of "normal" people. They can report the subject and call for something to be done about it, but this power is easily abused. The *Time* cyberporn article called for reform on the basis of Rimm's findings, proclaiming, "A new study shows us how pervasive and wild [pornography on the Internet] really is. Can we protect our kids—and free speech?" These cries to protect our children affected the likes of Senators James Exon and Robert Dole, who took the *Time* article with its "shocking" revelations (as well as a sample of pornographic images) to the Senate floor, appealing for changes to the law. From this response it is clear how powerful a magazine article can be, regardless of the integrity and accuracy of its reporting.

The *Time* article had all of Cohen's elements relating to the fueling of a moral panic: exaggeration, fallacies, and misleading pictures and titles. Because certain publications are highly regarded and enjoy an important role in society, anything printed in their pages is consumed and believed by a large audience. People accept what they read because, to the best of their knowledge, it is the truth. So, even though the *Time* article was based on a report by an undergraduate student passing as "a research team from Carnegie Mellon," the status of the magazine was great enough to launch a panic that continues unabated—from the halls of Congress to the pulpits of churches, from public schools to the offices of software developers, from local communities to the global village.

> *"A high percentage of non-incarcerated rapists and child molesters have said that they have been incited by pornography to commit crimes."*

Pornography Causes Violence

Diana E.H. Russell

Diana E.H. Russell is a sociologist specializing in the study of sexual violence against women and girls. In the following excerpt, taken from her book *Against Pornography: The Evidence of Harm*, she argues that pornography causes rape and other violence against women. The more pornography becomes available and accepted, Russell contends, the more desensitized people become to the violence and degradation portrayed in it. As a result, she claims that men grow more willing to commit acts of real violence against women.

As you read, consider the following questions:

1. What percentage of women in the Canadian experiment on pornography reported having been upset by requests to enact pornography, according to Russell?
2. According to the author, how much money does the pornography industry earn per year?
3. What analogy does Van White use to illustrate the degradation of women as a result of pornography?

Adapted from the Conclusion of *Against Pornography: The Evidence of Harm*, by Diana E.H. Russell (Berkeley, CA: Russell Publications, 1994), pp. 149–51. Copyright © 1993 by Diana E.H. Russell. Reprinted with permission.

I believe that my theory that pornography—both violent and non-violent—can cause rape, can be adapted to apply to other forms of sexual assault and abuse, as well as to woman battering and femicide (the misogyny-motivated killing of women). I have done the preliminary work on such an adaptation to the causal relationship between pornography and child sexual abuse and plan to publish this work in the future.

Porn Causes Violence

I believe that the rich and varied data now available to us from all kinds of sources, when considered together, strongly support my theory.

- A high percentage of non-incarcerated rapists and child molesters have said that they have been incited by pornography to commit crimes;
- Pre-selected normal healthy male students say they are more likely to rape a woman after just one exposure to violent pornography;
- A high percentage of male junior high school students, high school students, and adults in a non-laboratory survey report imitating X-rated movies within a few days of exposure;
- Hundreds of women have testified in public about how they have been victimized by pornography;
- Ten percent of a probability sample of 930 women in San Francisco and 25% of female subjects in an experiment on pornography in Canada reported having been upset by requests to enact pornography;
- Many prostitutes report that they have experienced pornography-related sexual assault;
- The laws of social learning must surely apply to pornography at least as much as to the mass media in general. Indeed, I—and others—have argued that sexual arousal and orgasm are likely to serve as unusually potent reinforcers of the message conveyed by pornography;
- A large body of experimental research has shown that the viewing of violent pornography results in higher rates of aggression against women by male subjects.

It is no wonder that Edward I. Donnerstein stated that the

relationship between pornography and violence against women is stronger than the relationship between smoking and lung cancer.

Desensitization

One of the effects of viewing non-violent pornography, discovered by Dolf Zillmann, is that "the more extensive the exposure, the more accepting of pornography subjects became." Although females expressed significantly less acceptance than males, this effect also applied to females. Pornography has expanded into a multi-billion-dollar-a-year industry, and I believe we are seeing on a massive scale some of the very effects so brilliantly and carefully documented in some of the experiments by Neil Malamuth, Donnerstein, Zillmann, and their colleagues. Donnerstein's description of the desensitization that occurred in healthy pre-selected male students after only five days of viewing woman-slashing films may apply to ever-growing segments of our society.

Ted Bundy and Pornography

"I take full responsibility for whatever I've done and all the things that I've done. The question and the issue is how this kind of [pornographic] literature contributed and helped mold and shape these kinds of violent behavior."

The pornographic images eventually broke down his "last vestiges of restraint—the barriers to actually doing something," Ted Bundy [who was executed in 1989 for the sex slaying of 12-year-old Kimberly Leach] said.

Associated Press, "Killer Seduced by Violence-Laden Porn," 1999.

Van White, the Chairperson of the Hearings on Pornography in Minnesota in 1983, commented as follows on the impact of the testimony by the survivors of pornography-related abuse:

These horror stories made me think of the history of slavery in this country—how Black women were at the bottom of the pile, treated like animals instead of human beings. As I listened to these victims of pornography, I heard young women describe how they felt about . . . the way women's genitals and breasts are displayed and women's bodies are shown in compromising postures. I thought about the time of slavery, when Black women had their bodies invaded, their teeth and limbs examined, their bodies checked out for breeding, checked out as you would an animal, and I said to myself, 'We've come a long way, haven't we?'

Today we have an industry . . . showing women in the same kind of submissive and animalistic roles.

United States' culture appears to have been affected by the very effects the research shows. The massive propaganda campaign is working; people now actually see differently. Pornography has to become increasingly extreme before people are disturbed by, or even notice, the violence and degradation portrayed in it. Very few see the real abuse that is happening to some of the women who are photographed. As Zillmann shows, "heavy consumption of common forms of pornography fosters an appetite for stronger materials." What was considered "hard-core" in the past has become soft-core in the present. Where will this all end? Will we as a culture forever refuse to read the writing on the wall?

"Pornography can serve as a mitigating factor in sexual violence. It provides a healthy release for those with pent up sexual frustration."

Pornography Does Not Cause Violence

Mathew Gever

Mathew Gever asserts in the following viewpoint that pornography does not cause violence. Moreover, he maintains that viewing pornography can prevent violence against women by releasing pent up sexual frustration in men. Gever contends that countries that have strict anti-porn laws report higher incidences of rape than do countries where pornography is easily accessible. Mathew Gever writes for the *Daily Bruin*, a student newspaper published on the University of California, Los Angeles campus.

As you read, consider the following questions:
1. Why is it impossible to objectively measure the impact of pornography on a person's actions, according to Gever?
2. How does Gever use the example of medieval Europe to help support his argument?
3. How does blaming pornography for violence against women affect the trials of those accused of sexual assault, according to the author?

Reprinted, with permission, from Mathew Gever, "Pornography Helps Women, Society," *Daily Bruin*, December 3, 1998.

Repressing sexuality seems to be a hallmark of our country. Whether it's the impeachment of Bill Clinton [who was accused of having an inappropriate sexual affair with a White House intern] or slapping letters of approval on movies, this nation finds it necessary to control issues of carnal knowledge.

Pornography as Scapegoat

Pornography falls under this paradigm. There is a false idea in our society that controlling pornography is somehow beneficial to us. Pornography is an issue that serves as a scapegoat for the ills of society. It is one of the few, if not the only, issues where religious reactionaries and radical feminists agree. The religious right blames it for moral bankruptcy while the militant feminist division blames it for the continued subjugation of women.

Both these arguments warrant a closer examination.

The religious right takes a stance against pornography in hopes of enforcing good Christian values among people. What this means is that people should not be having sex, and that women belong back in the kitchen baking pies and knitting sweaters.

Women Are No Smarter than Children?

Then there are the radical feminists, who regard pornography as an endangerment to women. What they argue is that women cannot possibly consent to sex, since we live in a male-dominated society which renders consent impossible. This has led to action by this bloc to impede any production of pornography.

One example of this is a Minneapolis anti-porn ordinance issued in 1983. This ordinance stated that all women who worked in porn were coerced and could sue the producers and distributors, whether or not the woman was of age, was fully aware of what she was doing and had signed a release. This ordinance claimed that women were incapable of rendering decisions for themselves and needed the government to protect them. The ordinance even stated that "Children are incapable of consenting to engage in pornographic conduct, even absent physical coercion and therefore require special protection. By the same token, the physical and psychological well-being of women ought to be afforded comparable protection."

So this is what hundreds of years of feminism has brought us to—women are no smarter than children.

Pornography Can Prevent Violence

Some anti-porn crusaders also argue that pornography poses a physical threat to women. They claim that the viewing of pornography leads to violence against women. A number of problems exist with this argument. First, there is no real method to objectively measure the impact of pornography on a person's actions. Sexual responses are endemic to the individual and cannot be accurately measured by a laboratory setting.

Also, pornography can serve as a mitigating factor in sexual violence. It provides a healthy release for those with pent-up sexual frustration. Who is going to sexually assault a person after they have just masturbated in their living room? Without this release, sexual frustration builds up and can easily manifest itself in the form of violence.

Research by The National Research Council's Panel on Understanding and Preventing Violence has shown that there is no demonstrated link between pornography and violence against women. Also, research by Larry Baron and Murray Straus has shown that there is a negative correlation between pornography and gender violence. For example, look at Iran and Saudi Arabia. Both have strict anti-pornography laws, yet they still have high instances of violence against women. Compare that with countries such as Denmark and Germany—in both countries pornography is readily accessible, yet they have some of the lowest rates of violence against women.

Videotapes Do Not Rape

Some may blame this discrepancy on cultural differences. But remember, Denmark produced the Vikings—and we all know what Germany was capable of—so it is wrong to say that violence is not a part of their cultures.

To further illustrate this point, look at Medieval Europe. This was a period when rape was at its highest levels. *Penthouse* magazine did not exist at this time. Neither did "Debbie Does Dallas" [a pornographic movie]. Yet violence against women persisted, since men did not have a safe place to release their sexual frustration.

The Missing Link

- No reputable research in the U.S., Europe or Asia finds a causal link between pornography and violence. Meese Commissioner [a commission established by Ronald Reagan in 1985 to study pornography] Dr. Judith Becker said "I've been working with sex offenders for 10 years, and have reviewed the scientific literature and I don't think a causal link exists."

- No research, including the Surgeon General's report, finds a link between "kinky" or "degrading" images and violence. Exposure to such material does not cause people to change their sexual preferences or commit acts against their will. The derailed impulses of child abusers and rapists are caused by childhood traumas. "They are not," wrote leading researcher John Money, "borrowed from movies, books or other people."

Patti O. Britton, Jennifer Maguire, and Beth Nathanson, "Feminism and Free Speech: Pornography," Feminists for Free Expression, 1993.

In addition, blaming pornography diffuses responsibility away from the culprit. Anyone tried for sexual assault can blame pornography and say that he was not in control of his actions. Videotapes do not rape, people do, and responsibility should be assigned as such.

Pornography Benefits Women

In fact, rather than harming women, pornography actually brings them a number of benefits. This is one of the few industries where women are paid more than men. Also, pornography allows for experimentation and breaks orthodox standards of sexuality. The idea of lying in the missionary position while counting the stars is flouted, and instead the enjoyment of sex is encouraged. Restricting pornography limits the choices that a woman has and invokes the repression of Victorian times.

This relates to another important point. Despite the common stereotype, the greatest number of people renting porn are couples. This is shown in the increase of "chick porn," which is pornography geared especially toward women. These media emphasize the female sexual experience and encourage couples to experiment. There is no violence or degradation, just people enjoying themselves.

Also, compare pornography to other things that are legally available, and see which is worse. For example, one can go to a Blockbuster video store and rent "Faces of Death," yet one can not rent the original version of "Showgirls."

I see the logic: watching animals getting disemboweled is healthy, whereas watching people voluntarily having sex is not.

In fact, our anti-porn laws have gotten so ridiculous that a law now exists that prevents the simulation of child pornography. This means that if the people involved appear to be under 18, the act is a crime.

The actors involved could both be 35, but if they look underage, the act is a crime.

Who decides whether they appear to be underage? Generally it is the government, abiding by another subjective law that has no concrete basis, but rather it exists on ambiguous criteria.

And do not forget the issue of freedom of expression. Pornography involves consenting adults who so choose to be involved in this field. The First Amendment does not say anything about protecting what is morally proper, but rather the choice of the individual to express himself or herself in whatever legal manner he or she pleases. For some, pornography is this means of expression. If one is offended by porn, do not watch or look at it. There is no law saying you have to. Therefore, it is no one's business to regulate what a person decides to do with his or her own body.

Anti-porn crusaders do nothing more than degrade women. By pushing for legislation, these factions serve to promote the idea that women cannot make decisions for themselves and need the protection of the patriarchal state.

> *"I was not a willing participant [in pornography]. There were guns, there were knives, there were beatings, there were threats on the lives of my family."*

Pornography Harms Those Involved in Its Production

Linda Marchiano

Linda Marchiano appeared as Linda Lovelace in the pornographic film *Deep Throat*. She is also the author of *Ordeal*, an account of her experiences in the pornography industry. In the following viewpoint, which is excerpted from testimony before the Attorney General's Commission on Pornography (the Meese Commission), Marchiano describes being coerced into participating in pornography by means of mental abuse, beatings, and threats against herself and her family. Marchiano insists that although she appears to be enjoying herself in *Deep Throat*, she was in fact brutalized and traumatized during the film's production.

As you read, consider the following questions:

1. What does Marchiano say happened the first three times she tried to escape from Charles Trainor?
2. How does Marchiano explain the fact that she appears to enjoy herself in the film?

Excerpted from Linda Marchiano's testimony before the Attorney General's Commission on Pornography, January 21, 1986, New York, N.Y.

It all began in 1971. I was recuperating from a near-fatal automobile accident at my parents' home in Florida. A girlfriend of mine came over to visit me with a person by the name of Mr. Charles Trainor. Mr. Trainor came off as a very considerate gentleman, asking us what we would like to do and how we would like to spend our time and our afternoons, opening doors and lighting cigarettes and doing all the so-called good manners of society. Needless to say, I was impressed and started to date him.

I was not at the time getting along with my parents. I was twenty-one-years-old and was resenting being told to be home at 11:00 and to call and say where I was and give them the number and address.

The Biggest Mistake

Here comes the biggest mistake of my life. Seeing how upset I was with my home life, Mr. Trainor offered his assistance. He said I could come and live at his house in north Miami. The relationship at this time was platonic, which was just fine with me. My plan was to recuperate and to go back to New York and live the life that I was living before my accident.

I thought then that he was being kind and a nice friend. Today I know why the relationship was platonic. He was incapable of any kind of sexual act without inflicting some kind of degradation or pain on another human being. When I decided to head back for home and informed Mr. Trainor of my intention, that was when I met the real Mr. Trainor and my two and a half years of imprisonment began. He beat me physically and mentally from that day forward. He made a complete turnaround. I literally became a complete prisoner of his. I was not allowed out of sight or allowed to use a bathroom without his permission. When speaking to either my friends or my parents, he was on the extension with his Walther PPK .45 automatic 8-shot pointed at me.

The Ordeal of Pornography

I was beaten physically and suffered mental abuse each and every day. In my book *Ordeal*, which is an autobiography, I go into greater detail of the atrocities that I was put through, from prostitution to porno films to celebrity satisfier. The things that he used to get me involved in pornography ranged from this PPK Walther .45 automatic 8-shot and an M-16 semiautomatic machine gun to threats on the lives of my friends and my family. I have seen the kind of people involved in pornography and how they will use anyone to get what they want.

The coldness and the callousness that they possess is immense. So many people asked me why I didn't escape. Well, I did, because I am here today. I did try, during my two and a half years, to escape, on three separate occasions. The first and second time I suffered a brutal beating for trying. The third time I was at my parents' house, and Mr. Trainor came over and he said that if I didn't go with him he would kill my parents and I said that, no, he wouldn't do that, and he said that I will shoot every member of your "blank" family as they come through the door. And then at that time my nephew came crawling into the room, and I got up and left with Mr. Trainor.

Lucky to Stay Sane

From the age of four to sixteen, I was used in pornographic magazines and films. My father, his friends, my uncles, and my grandfather made pornography using my mother, myself and numerous other women and children. . . . My father and his allies spent years training me. They trained me like you train a dog, a puppy, only I was much less than a dog. . . . Next to nothing. . . . Nothing at all. The bright lights and the pictures for sale of my pain, my pain shattered like glass. A thousand pieces, a thousand printings of the rapes. Immortalized. Eternal. Sold, laughed at, . . . fantasized over, and the profit went to my father, my uncles, my grandfather and I was lucky if I got food and I was lucky to stay alive and I was lucky to stay sane.

Anonymous, *Off Our Backs*, April 1993.

Some of you might say that I was foolish for going with Mr. Trainor, but I am not the kind of a person that could have lived the rest of my life knowing that it was possible because somebody else's life was taken.

After three unsuccessful attempts at escaping, I realized that I had to create a so-called master plan. It took six months of preparation convincing Mr. Trainor that I thought what he was saying was right, that beating people was the right thing to do, that abusing humans was proper, that pornography was great.

Fortunately for me, after six months I acquired fifteen minutes out of his presence, but I also had someone who wanted to help me.

I tried to tell my story several times, once to Vern Scott, who is a UPI reporter, and he told me that he couldn't print it. I also tried to tell a program in California what had happened to me, and they just changed the subject.

After my final escape, I was hiding out and I also tried to call the Beverly Hills Police Department, and I asked them to do something. I tried to tell them my story, and they told me to call back when he was in the room with his .45 or his M-16. I was brought up on obscenity charges in California.

A grand jury watched the film [*Deep Throat*] while I tried to black out what I was seeing and remembering and feeling the day that film was being shot.

After they asked me why I did it, I told them that a gun was influencing me, and they said, "Oh." No charges were filed against Mr. Trainor, and I was acquitted because it was done against my will.

Somehow pornography has brought me here today. All I can do is tell you my story and what happened to me. I was a victim of pornography.

Not a Willing Participant

Dr. Park Dietz: You mentioned several details about the firearms involved. Why did you mention the details about them?

Marchiano: Well, because I think it's very important for people to know that I was not a willing participant. There were guns, there were knives, there were beatings, there were threats on the lives of my family constantly, and after the physical abuse, the mental abuse becomes just as damaging. I just think it's important that people realize that. So many people that produce these types of films will say, Well, we check out and make sure that these women are doing it willingly.

But you know, I always ask them, had Mr. Trainor come with Linda Lovelace ten years ago, would you have known that she was an unwilling participant? So how can they say that they make sure all the women are there willingly?

Dietz: It's been said that the behavior that you evidenced in the film *Deep Throat* looks to others as being inconsistent with one being coerced. I wonder if you would care to comment on how that came about.

Marchiano: Well, I learned very quickly with Mr. Trainor to do exactly what I was told to do and do it to the best of my ability and to be convincing, because if I did become emotional, I ended up crying, or, you know, not looking like I was really enjoying myself, and then I suffered a brutal beating, some kind of sexual perversion as punishment, and I would have to do it anyway. So my mother didn't raise me as a total fool. I realized what I would have to do is be convincing and do it and get it over with. That whole film was done in that way. Everything was done just one time.

Dietz: Did you undergo any beatings during the course of the filming?

Marchiano: Yes, as a matter of fact, after the first day of shooting I suffered a brutal beating in my room, and the whole crew of the film was in the next room.

There was a door joining the rooms, and we were in this room, they were in this room, and Mr. Trainor started pushing me around and punching me. I was smiling on the set too much that day, and then he started bouncing me off the walls and kicking me.

Well, I figured, if all these people were in the other room, maybe now somebody will help me. I will scream for help. And the only thing that happened was the room became very silent, and that was it.

The next day, they listened to him continue to beat me—and the next day the greatest complaint was I had a couple of bruises on my leg. You brought up the smile in *Deep Throat*, but nobody ever asked me how did I get those bruises, where did those bruises come from, how did they get there. Everybody always says, "Well, you got there, you smiled, you looked like you were having a good time." That smile is what saved my life.

Dietz: What was done to cover up the bruises?

Marchiano: One of the guys that was on the film, Mr. Reams, was also into stage makeup and all that, and he had the right kind of pancake or whatever they do. They just put layers and layers on it to try to cover it, but it still shows through.

"I have never been forced or coerced to do anything that I did not want to do."

Pornography Does Not Harm Those Involved in Its Production

Melissa Monet

Melissa Monet is a writer, producer, and director of adult films. In the following viewpoint, Monet argues that jobs in the pornography industry are satisfying, safe, and lucrative. She dispels the notion that those involved in making pornography are abused, claiming that she was never forced to do anything she didn't want to do. She contends that the sex-crazed characters in pornographic films are not accurate representations of the average people who play them.

As you read, consider the following questions:

1. According to Monet, approximately how many male sex performers work in the pornography industry?
2. How many adult sex performers have contracted HIV, according to the author?
3. In the author's opinion, what are two reasons that adult sex performers might abuse drugs?

Reprinted, with permission, from Melissa Monet, "Phallic Fallacies and Ball Blunders," *Gauntlet*, vol. 2, 1997.

I have always wondered what goes through people's minds when they make assumptions about other human beings and the choices they make. As a former adult performer (oh, how politically correct of me), and now a full-fledged pornographer, I have experienced the gamut of misconceptions about an industry of which I am still in awe.

I have been very lucky; I chose to enter the porno industry a little later in life than some of my peers, thus helping me to avoid some of the pitfalls of a sometimes misogynistic business (the ladies know that this pertains to all businesses). I have been dismayed, however to learn the outside world's ideas of who or what we are and what makes us tick.

The Moral Majority would have you believe that we are a bunch of fornicating rabbits, possessed by the devil himself. I receive several letters a month at my fan club address from Bible thumpers and lunatics (although I believe they are one and the same), begging me to repent my evil ways and to find God. . . . I didn't know I had lost him. It's amazing that religion, not the belief in God, has done more to fuck up people's minds, caused more wars, and is associated with more sex crimes than pornography could ever have caused. Oh, the hypocrisy!

Fans, on the other hand, are very happy that we are a randy group, even though most of them think that our sexual prowess is beyond the capabilities of normal people. Nymphomaniacs and super studs with twelve inch penises are commonly, if fallaciously, thought of as what makes up the performers' pool. With the average penis size in porn being about seven inches, it's a far cry from the monstrosities that [men supposedly have]. Nor are the men in the industry the long lasting, hard men that viewers enjoy watching through the help of movie magic and good editing. Some of the guys have a hard time getting erections and others have trouble ejaculating on cue. But let's see how well a challenger would do with twenty-five people staring and laughing at you while waiting on wood (an erection). And even though the porno industry is filled with eager sex performers who enjoy their work, I have yet to meet a clinical nymphomaniac. I find that most of the women in porn are just open-minded free spirits that chose a career that has few boundaries and lots of perks, and the guys, well, they just want to get laid.

So, of course, when people ask me what it is like to have sex with so many different men, I just have to laugh at the assumption. There are very few male sex performers in the adult industry. I can barely think of fifteen, and I would be hard pressed to come up with twenty-five overall. Most of the women in the industry have a list of men that they work with, and that list is usually very short. In the upper echelons of the business there are less than ten men performing; the same ten men that you see in almost every feature (a movie with a story and a little bit of production value). The reason there are so few men is that it isn't easy to perform in front of a camera. That's also why the men who *can* perform have such longevity.

The more popular men in the industry have sex with numerous members of the female talent pool, but I think that it is the most thankless job in the business. Which brings me to the strange observation that some people have; namely that I should feel used and abused in such a male dominated business (apparently they haven't seen me perform). I am a top (a dominatrix), a type A personality. I have never been forced or coerced to do anything that I did not want to do, but it's usually the men that feel used. They don't sell the movie, so they don't get much recognition. They're a prop, a penis without a face. Hell, if it weren't for the fact that they get the bulk of the dialogue, you wouldn't even see their faces half the time. Twice the work at half the pay . . . but lots of babes. Where else can you get laid and get paid? And the pay is still more than what you make in a nine to fiver. Sounds like a good deal to me.

But there is a drawback—the fear of disease. Sexually Transmitted Diseases (STD's) infections, herpes, hepatitis and HIV [which leads to AIDS] are some of the things that the performers worry about every day. STD's and various other infections are easy to detect and to cure; none of them being life threatening. They are treated immediately and then dismissed.

As of 1997, there have been three known performers who have contracted the HIV virus. All three were exposed *outside* of the industry, and when they were tested in order to work, the results came up HIV positive. Stringent blood testing detected the virus within a short window period, preventing exposure to the other members of the industry.

Several panics ago, there were a few performers with inconclusive tests; this softened the blow for the performers that have since come up positive. Panic is more fearful than the virus itself. The lack of education fueled the fire that caused a lot of the performers to accuse each other of exposing them to the virus, but so far to date, none of the three have infected anyone else in the industry.

Just a Job

Ginger put herself through New York University performing in peepshows and maintains that the shows are innocuous fun. "It's a safe, harmless way to have some erotica in one's life. It is certainly victimless and should be accepted in society." . . . Many people in the porn business say the performers are just people working a job. Alan, who owns a peep emporium, . . . says the women come from many walks of life. "There are a lot of college girls, women that have straight professions."

Wes Goodman, *USA Today*, March 1994.

You're in porn? Wow! You don't seem to be a dumb bimbo. I can't blame people for believing this to be true—after all, we are portrayed as the stupidest women on the planet. Well, what do you expect to see? We are told all the time that men want to marry an intelligent woman, but they want to boff the dumb bimbo, so a lot of the scripts are written for the male fantasy. How else could you explain an ugly guy getting the babe of his dreams with a line like, "Hey, wanna fuck?" In porn, the girl always says yes. Talk about your break from reality. In real life, the girl would kick you in the balls.

Just to set the record straight, we do have our share of dumb women and even dumber men, but I have found the majority of the performers come from many different walks of life and have varying educational backgrounds. Still, even a diversified bunch of burnt-out corporate types and a few Rhodes Scholars cannot erase the bimbo image.

Probably the worst misconception is that we were all

abused as children. This is an odd industry in that it attracts a lot of lost souls, but most of the performers are just searching for the almighty dollar. I have noticed in the past that there are fewer victims of abuse in this industry than I have found in the corporate world (unless you count the over-achieving dropouts that inhabit most of the business end of this wonderful industry).

Performers from abusive backgrounds don't usually last long, finding this work too cold and clinical for their needs. Some of them will turn to drugs or alcohol to ease the pain from a lonely or abusive childhood; others will grin and bare it.

And what would the porn industry be without drugs? Beats me. I have never seen a business that didn't have its share of drug and alcohol abusers. The majority of the adult industry is clean and sober; some having been there, done that, others never even taking an interest in experimenting. Now, that's not to say that there aren't drug and alcohol abusers. Just like everywhere else, and I mean *everywhere*, there are people who never got the opportunity to have money, or even a modicum of fame, and those are two very strong ingredients for an excuse to get hooked.

The other excuses that people in the adult industry could use for drinking and doing drugs are:

(1) They are pariahs to everyone around them. Sure, some people on the outside think it's a cool job, but I bet their families aren't among them.

(2) It is very hard to have a normal relationship with someone on the outside of the industry. How many men or women can accept their partner [making porno films] for a living? It's a rare find indeed. That's why so many of the performers find solace with one another.

(3) Growing up with a strong religious background and having that wonderful guilt thing creeping up on them has done a little damage, too.

(4) And the strongest excuse for some of the girls is so that they can gather up the courage to perform or to dance on the road. The guys use it for courage too, but unfortunately it always has the opposite effect. Once a performer is known to have a problem, an attempt at intervention by either a

peer or a loved one usually occurs, or the performer will eventually become so bad that they are blacklisted until they clean up their act. Just like any other job, if they redeem themselves by proving they are once again reliable, they are taken back into the fold. I would like to clear up one major misconception that has always bothered me personally—being lumped in with child pornographers by virtue of the fact that we are in an adult related industry. As an industry, pornography is for consenting adults only, regulated by the performers, manufacturers, distributors, and the government. The adult industry does not condone nor promote child pornography in any way, and we abhor anyone who partakes in such practices. The adult entertainment industry has taken many steps to help eradicate child pornography on the Internet, as well as regulating its own web sites to keep sexually curious, underage children from accessing adult material. Net Nanny and other such programs [that block obscene material] have proven to be very effective.

The government is constantly regulating the adult industry under the guise of protecting children, piggy backing anti-pornography and free speech laws on the back of child pornography bills. The government's use of this ploy is effective because none of us want to vote against a children's issue. It's unfortunate that most people are not aware that the adult industry lobbies to protect *everyone's* rights each time such a bill comes up. Yes, it affects the adult industry directly, but it also affects everyone's constitutional rights as well.

There are bills that are supposed to protect the public from pornography that go to the extreme where an adult, in the privacy of his or her own home, could be arrested for certain acts outside the confines of the law's definition of normal sex. Watch out, Big Brother is watching you.

Now the government has gone even further in its regulating of what we see and do. By eliminating the adult-oriented broadcasting of [channels that feature pornography such as] Spice and Playboy before 10:00 P.M., the government is hoping to keep children from watching sex on television. Yet there is more genitalia and sex shown on the more public channels than on the heavily regulated and pay-per-view adult-only channels. There is absolutely no correlation between the adult industry and child pornography, or bestiality for that matter, either. And although money, not morality, is the driving force of the sex business, we police ourselves quite well, following the guidelines of our laws to the letter.

I would like to add that I do not feel that child pornographers are human beings. They are cowards, thus they have no rights, and should not be allowed to hide behind the veil of freedom of speech. But hey, that's just my opinion.

So, whatever you may think about the porno industry and the people in it, remember, try not to judge us based on the few individuals that you might have seen on the *Jerry Springer Show* (it's rigged anyway) or heard on Howard Stern. Just realize that this is a business made up of individuals trying to make a buck and to give the public what it wants, good, clean, old fashioned . . . SEX!

Periodical Bibliography

The following articles have been selected to supplement the diverse views presented in this chapter. Addresses are provided for periodicals not indexed in the *Readers' Guide to Periodical Literature*, the *Alternative Press Index*, the *Social Sciences Index*, or the *Index to Legal Periodicals and Books*.

Jim Cusack	"The Murky World of Internet Porn," *World Press Review*, November 1996.
Trip Gabriel	"New Issue at Work: On-Line Sex Sites," *The New York Times*, June 27, 1996.
Holman W. Jenkins Jr.	"Porn Again? An Industry Fantasizes About Respect," *Wall Street Journal*, April 1, 1998.
Ann E. Menasche	"An Interview with Diana Russell: Violence, Pornography, and Woman Hating," *Against the Current*, July/August 1997.
Gabriel Rotello	"That's Sexertainment," *Advocate*, March 28, 2000.
Eric Schlosser	"The Business of Pornography," *U.S. News & World Report*, February 10, 1997.
Roger Scruton	"Very Safe Sex," *National Review*, July 28, 1997.
John Simons	"The Web's Dirty Secret," *U.S. News & World Report*, August 19, 1996.
Lynn Snowden	"Deep Inside the Valley of Sin," *George*, March 1998. Available from 1633 Broadway, 41st Floor, New York, NY 10019.
Joel Stein	"Porn Goes Mainstream," *Time*, September 7, 1998.
Mark Stewart	"Sex Saturated Culture Sends Message to Kids," *Insight*, May 22, 2000. Available from 3600 New York Ave. NE, Washington, DC 20002.
Chitaporn Vanaspong	"Dangerous Chat: Stopping the Spread of Child Pornography on the Internet," *Toward Freedom*, Winter 1998/99.

Should Pornography Be Censored?

Chapter Preface

A 1992 decision by the Canadian Supreme Court—often referred to as the Butler decision—expanded Canada's legal definition of obscenity and made it illegal to import or distribute any printed or visual material that was "degrading" or "harmful" to women.

Many Americans look to Canada's decision in the Butler case as a model for modifying U.S. obscenity laws. Supporters of censorship contend that hardcore pornography, because it degrades women, is destructive speech and is therefore not protected by the First Amendment. Such obscenity should be censored to protect women, they maintain. Others who oppose pornography argue that prohibiting the distribution of obscene materials is not censorship at all. According to Betty Wein, who works as an editor for *Morality in the Media*, an organization that works to stop the traffic in pornography, the legal meaning of censorship is "prior restraint of First Amendment rights by government." Since obscenity is not protected by the First Amendment, she argues, confiscating obscene materials is not an act of censorship.

However, many Americans criticize the Butler decision. They contend that it allows government officials to define morality for everyone. If a similar law were enacted in the United States, they maintain, it would erode First Amendment rights. Many who oppose censorship of pornography agree that pornography harms women, but they argue that censorship would harm them more by allowing government officials to make decisions about women's welfare without their consent. In addition, critics maintain that censorship laws often target those who threaten the status quo. The novelist Dorothy Allison claims that "the majority of the books being stopped at the [Canadian] border are from small feminist, gay and other alternative presses."

The Butler decision has intensified the debate about the benefits and dangers of government regulation of pornography. The authors in the following viewpoints argue whether or not pornography should be censored.

> "[The 'evil' of censorship] does not even come close to standing by indifferently while the culture is debased by the influence of porn merchants our grandparents would have sent to jail."

Pornography Should Be Censored

James K. Fitzpatrick

James K. Fitzpatrick writes for the *Wanderer*, a Catholic weekly newspaper. In the following viewpoint, Fitzpatrick contends that it is better to censor pornography than to allow it to debase U.S. culture. He maintains that in the past, those who dealt in pornography had to do so in secret in order to avoid shame and punishment. He claims, however, that today pornography is publicly consumed, and those who want to censor it have gone into hiding.

As you read, consider the following questions:
1. According to Fitzpatrick, what did his coworkers do with their pornography in the 1960s and 1970s?
2. What famous case defined U.S. censorship laws, according to Fitzpatrick?
3. According to the author, what is the legal definition of obscenity?

Reprinted, with permission, from James K. Fitzpatrick, "Plain Brown Wrappers," *The Wanderer*, May 13, 1999.

M any depressing things bobbed to the surface in the wake of the 1999 Columbine High School shootings in Littleton, Colorado, that left fifteen dead. One is the breadth of the liberal victory on the censorship question. It seemed as if every observer who condemned the music industry for feeding the fantasies of the two teenage shooters felt obliged to preface his comments with the disclaimer: "Now, let me stress I'm not calling for censorship."

But tell me: Why not? What is so ghastly about censorship? When did this anti-censorship fervor become the new American consensus? Even [Republican presidential hopeful] Pat Buchanan tempered his remarks by stressing that he was talking only about using the "presidential bully pulpit" against the likes of Marilyn Manson. Come on, Pat. You can do better than that. [Democratic vice president] Al Gore could have made that comment, while picking up campaign donations from a gathering of music industry executives.

Censorship: American as Apple Pie

Censorship is as American as apple pie. Abraham Lincoln's America would not have allowed Marilyn Manson's music to be sold over the counter. Neither would Teddy Roosevelt's, nor Harry Truman's, nor Dwight Eisenhower's. They would not have allowed rap music about gang raping coeds, either. They would not have given it a second thought. Garbage belongs in the garbage can.

The point is that you do not have to go back to the Dark Ages to find a time when Americans thought it entirely proper to limit the influence of sleaze merchants.

I grew up in the 1950s in the playgrounds of New York City. There was porn on those playgrounds. But it was brought around by characters who looked as if they lived under a rock, and they displayed their wares behind the handball courts while looking over their shoulders to see if any authority figures were in the vicinity. The stuff was illegal, and they knew it, usually something one of their uncles picked up in the bowels of the city.

I worked in factories and with a tree company that cleared the limbs from around the power lines in the 1960s and 1970s. There were people I worked with who had porn. But it was shipped to them in nondescript envelopes, with return addresses to publishers no one ever heard of, with names like "Acme Press" and "Artists' Studios." Not quite plain brown wrappers, but it was an apt metaphor.

In the factories they would keep the material buried in the back of their lockers. One of the drivers for the tree company (one of the most bizarre men I have ever met; his parole officer agreed) routinely stashed a few of his favorites in a spring under the front seat of our truck.

Censoring Pornography Does Not Harm Freedom of Opinion

If we start censoring pornography and obscenity, shall we not inevitably end up censoring political opinion? A lot of people seem to think this would be the case—which only shows the power of doctrinaire thinking over reality. We had censorship of pornography and obscenity for 150 years, until almost yesterday, and I am not aware that freedom of opinion in this country was in any way diminished as a consequence of this fact.

Irving Kristol, *Society*, September/October 1999.

Now, remember, this was not that long ago. I can't give you a detailed account of how graphic these magazines were. (Years of lectures by Marist brothers [a Roman Catholic teaching order] and Jesuit priests had instilled in me a sense of guilt about looking at such things. For which I am still grateful.) But I would be willing to bet that they were no worse than what teenagers can rent at the local video store in many cities these days.

But, I repeat, it was illegal to sell and distribute such material in this country at that time, just a few decades ago. As a matter of fact, it probably still is, if our officials had the backbone to enforce the laws on the books. I haven't read anywhere that the *Miller v. California* (1973) case has been overruled.

Obscenity Laws

The Miller case, you will recall, defined the country's obscenity laws. It established three guidelines. To be obscene—and subject to censorship—the material in question has to be sexually explicit and appeal to prurient interests. It can have no redeeming social or artistic value. It has to offend prevailing community standards of decency. If that does not describe Marilyn Manson's act, what does?

If a book or movie meets these standards it is not entitled to protection under the First Amendment guarantees of freedom of speech and press. It can be prohibited—censored—by local governments. In other words, Marilyn Manson's rock videos and "gangsta" rap CDs and the Triple X movies they stack in the "Adult" section of your video rental store could be censored—if the local authorities were willing to make the effort.

They are not censored because local authorities have decided to look the other way; because they don't want to make a "big deal" about this stuff; or, most likely, because they have been browbeaten by the media and academic elites, who react as if censorship is the vilest activity a society can undertake.

Well, it is not. It does not even come close to standing by indifferently while the culture is debased by the influence of porn merchants our grandparents would have sent to jail and our great-grandparents would have ridden out of town on a rail, maybe with a veneer of tar and feathers.

"Keeping people from thinking is exactly what censorship is really for."

Pornography Should Not Be Censored

Avedon Carol

Avedon Carol argues in the following viewpoint that opponents of pornography incorrectly claim that pornography causes harm. Censoring pornography, Carol claims, simply prohibits people from judging for themselves pornography's effects. Carol maintains that censorship has always been used to silence opposition. When public debate is shut down by censorship, Carol asserts, people cannot find solutions to real social problems. Avedon Carol is a founding member of Feminists Against Censorship, an organization whose goal is to fight censorship, including the censorship of pornography.

As you read, consider the following questions:
1. How did politicians suppress the women's liberation movement, according to Carol?
2. In the author's opinion, how did moral rightists smear sexual media?
3. How does Carol characterize the backgrounds of serial killers and child molesters?

Reprinted, with permission, from Avedon Carol, "Censorship? Just Say 'No!'" 1999, from the Gemini Site at http://rene.efa.org.au/censor/pcontrov.html.

For me, the question of censorship was simplified a long time ago when I noticed that pro-civil rights activists were being censored in the United States on the grounds of "obscenity." Given the complex sexual mythology that has always haunted American racial relations, it struck me as a sneaky trick to make part of the back-room ideology of racism impossible to confront in a public forum.

Censorship and Civil Rights

It wasn't new, of course. The first uses of the obscenity laws in America had been blatantly political, and the blues had been banned in Memphis as part of the suppression of black culture.

But the problem became increasingly obvious as the women's liberation movement in the late 1960s and early '70s was subjected to one anti-obscenity campaign after another. The primary targets seemed to be traditional—as always, pro-censorship forces were quick to go after material dealing specifically with women's health and reproductive issues. But everything from lesbianism to orgasm was up for discussion in the women's movement—all had been mythologised, and all played a role in the difficult relationships between men and women—and repressive politicians wanted to make sure we couldn't talk about those very things. The excuse was that those things weren't really "political"—they were "obscene."

Censorship and Sex

Obviously, people want to talk about sex, think about sex, play with sex and understand sex. Not just the mechanics of reproductive acts, either—we're after the whole nine yards. In the 1960s, the people who most wanted to talk about these things were teenagers and young adults, and our parents really didn't want us to. A lot has been said about how baby-boomers "think they invented sex," but the truth is that in a culture that never really talked about the subject in any substantive terms, our generation really did have to start from scratch in many ways. We're still inventing sex as a subject for public discussion.

Sex continues to be the first and most compelling point of

attack for moral rightists and career repressives. But as they found they couldn't evoke the Pavlovian fear response to mere mentions of sex anymore, they stepped up the rhetoric to smear sexual media with charges of violence and abuse of children. It's no longer sex, but "sex-&-violence"; no longer sexual acts, but "torture"; no longer porn, but "child porn."

It's a phoney dodge.

Reprinted by permission of Steve Artley, © 1989.

When feminists first brought up the subject of domestic violence and abuse, the American moral right was adamantly opposed to any movement to stamp these things out. Violence, they said, was a matter for families, not the state. Yet they are eager to see the state control non-abusive, consensual behaviour.

British moral rightists now unabashedly assert on national television (Newsnight, BBC2), that if people practice sadomasochistic (SM) sex they become child abusers. Merely "looking at explicit erotic media" (pornography), they say, turns men into abusers. Embarrassingly, our media presenters are too ignorant to question those claims.

In a highly-politicised debate where one side gets to control the discourse by censoring the subject at hand, they can say anything they want. If people never really get to see pornography, they won't know that it is less violent than other media, so the moral right can get away with claiming pornography is more violent. In this climate, it becomes difficult to point out that half a century of research and accumulated data conclusively proves that sexual openness and explicit media are not the problem. Question the moral right's position and they call you a child abuser.

If you look at the backgrounds of serial killers and child molesters, you rarely find that their parents were free love–practising hippies or porn-reading SM fans. They aren't gay rights activists or free speech advocates. The material they quote from isn't pornography or *The Blade* [a gay and lesbian newspaper]. . . . It's the *Bible*.

A Dangerous Weapon

History teaches that censorship is a dangerous weapon in the hands of government. Inevitably, it is used against those who want to change society, be they feminists, civil rights demonstrators or gay liberationists. Obscenity laws, especially, have been used to suppress information and art dealing with female sexuality and reproduction. Thus, the growing influence of anti-pornography feminism threatens to undermine long-established principles of free speech.

ACLU, Department of Public Education, December 11, 1994.

Sex and sexuality are fundamentals of the relationships—and confusions—between men and women. But it's only one example of a subject where problems have been made intractable by suppression of one side of the discourse. A closer look at problems related to crime and drugs shows that in most cases the sensible options have been discarded before the public debate is even permitted to take place. Our educational methodology has slipped where creative solutions have been thrown out. Our approaches to racial issues and economic policies are stagnant to the point of self-destruction because some things just cannot be said. We no longer feel free to question the received wisdom.

The beauty of the internet, for me, is that it creates a

place to express—and expose—all those suppressed views and ideas. It's a resource where students can examine a multiplicity of positions and arguments and sort them out for themselves. It invites you to think.

Ironically, however, the academic servers in Britain were the first to succumb to the fear of such debate and to impose censorship on Usenet groups [online discussion groups on a variety of topics]. It won't surprise me if similar controls end up being imposed on web searches. It will be a true victory for the most powerful and repressive forces if this tool, with all its potential, is crippled for those who want and need it most.

But then, keeping people from thinking is exactly what censorship is really for.

> *"It is because of porn's need to dehumanize women that it should not be an unhindered free speech issue."*

Censoring Pornography Would Benefit Women

John P. Araujo

In the following viewpoint, John P. Araujo argues that pornography should be censored because it dehumanizes women and diminishes their contributions to society. The right to free speech is not absolute, he contends, and speech can be censored when it harms society, as pornography does. John P. Araujo is a columnist for the *University Wire*.

As you read, consider the following questions:
1. In Araujo's opinion, what has been responsible for the increased popularity of pornography in recent times?
2. What example does the author provide of speech that is not protected by the right to free speech?
3. In the author's opinion, how does pornography dehumanize women?

Reprinted, with permission, from John P. Araujo, "Free Speech Should Not Cover Porn," *Texas Christian University Daily Skiff*, April 12, 2000.

P rostitution is said to be the world's oldest profession, but pornography is surely among the top three. We can try our best to rid society of porn, but it will continue to exist in some form or fashion as it always has—usually in "red-light districts" and in the shadows and corners of society.

Mainstream Pornography

Now, however, pornography has become more "mainstream" by spreading into a new area that has been rapidly gaining popularity in recent years: the Internet. Rare are the key words that you can type in Internet searches that will not produce a link to some kind of porn.

This increased access to porn has reintroduced the topic of the First Amendment rights of porn in our country. A classmate gave a report stating her opposition to porn as a First Amendment right.

She brought in pictures of porn that she obtained off the Internet (thus demonstrating how easy it is to get), but—instead of bringing pictures of women, she brought in pictures of men. This was to illustrate to the men (the usual "customers") how ugly porn is and how it felt to have your sex portrayed pornographically. I couldn't have thought of a better way of illustrating both of those points.

There are many people I know who thoroughly hate pornography, but—much to their reluctance—they acknowledge it as a First Amendment right.

The Right to Free Speech Is Not Absolute

The right to free speech should rightly be difficult to obstruct, but it is not absolute (as demonstrated in the classic "yelling 'fire' in a crowded theater when there is no fire" scenario). I have always had difficulty calling porn a free speech issue, and my classmate's presentation helped to clarify that for me even more.

Pornography serves no useful purpose, and worse, it does incalculable damage to society in how it portrays women. Men, too, are portrayed in porn, but women are still, by far, portrayed much more. The rise of Internet use and pornography comes when the contributions that women have made to society have been increasingly (and rightfully) acknowledged.

Pornography Harms Women

The proliferation of pornography becomes "two steps back" for every step forward that women take. How can we as a society continue to accept pornography as an unhindered free speech issue when it helps retard the progress women have made in society?

The Impact of Pornography on Women

When your rape is entertainment, your worthlessness is absolute. You have reached the nadir of social worthlessness. The civil impact of pornography on women is staggering, it keeps us socially silent, it keeps us socially compliant, it keeps us afraid in neighborhoods; and it creates a vast hopelessness for women, a vast despair. One lives inside a nightmare of sexual abuse that is both actual and potential, and you have the great joy of knowing that your nightmare is someone else's freedom and someone else's fun.

Andrea Dworkin, National Coalition for the Protection of Children and Families, January 22, 1986.

Art and science can portray a nude female without robbing her of her dignity and humanity, but pornographers must reduce women into tools of sexual satisfaction in order for women to suit their purposes. It is because of porn's need to dehumanize women that it should not be an unhindered free speech issue.

While making porn illegal will be no more successful in eliminating it than Prohibition was in eliminating alcohol consumption, I still believe that we should not make it so easy for pornographers to peddle their wares. We should not give porn the extent of free speech protection that we give to someone who is trying to expose political corruption or civil rights abuses.

Women deserve better than the efforts we have been putting out for them. Women do not deserve the in-your-face double standard of saying that we value their contributions to our society while we defend the portrayal of them as sex objects in pornography as a First Amendment right.

We can, and we must, do better than that.

> *"Pornography brings benefits to women. In censoring pornography, the state will impoverish rather than enrich them."*

Censoring Pornography Would Harm Women

Wendy McElroy

Wendy McElroy is the former president of Feminists for Free Expression/Canada and author of the book, *XXX: A Woman's Right to Pornography*. In the following viewpoint, McElroy argues that censoring pornography would harm women. Censoring pornography would allow the government to dictate what sexual practices are appropriate for women, she claims, and would reduce women to the status of children by questioning their ability to make decisions about their bodies. Moreover, McElroy asserts that censoring pornography would do nothing to stop rape because pornography has never been proven to be a cause of violence against women.

As you read, consider the following questions:

1. In McElroy's opinion, how should women who are against pornography protest its use?
2. Why is it so difficult to determine pornography's impact on behavior, according to the author?
3. According to the author, how did government oppress women in centuries past?

Abridged from Wendy McElroy, *Banning Pornography Endangers Women*, a pamphlet published by the International Society for Individual Liberty (1997), at www.seventhquest.net/isil.org/pamphlet/porno.htm. Reprinted with permission.

Why is pornography viewed as violence . . . and not merely words or images? This view was well embodied in the . . . Minneapolis anti-porn ordinance of 1983. The ordinance stated that all women who worked in porn were coerced, and could bring a civil lawsuit against producers and distributors. Coercion was deemed to be present even if the woman was of age, she fully understood the nature of the performance, she signed a contract and release, there were witnesses, she was under no threat, and she was fully paid.

Women and Consent

Consent by the woman was rendered impossible. The author of the Ordinance, anti-porn activist and radical feminist Catharine MacKinnon, later explained that "in the context of unequal power (between the sexes), one needs to think about the meaning of consent—whether it is a meaningful concept at all." A male-controlled society made it impossible for women to consent. Women who thought they agreed were so damaged by male society that they were not able to give true consent.

In over a decade of defending pornography against such attacks, I have avoided First Amendment arguments and preferred to challenge the anti-porn zealots on their own terms. The key questions became: Are women coerced into pornography? and How does porn relate to general societal violence against women? A secondary—but essential—question was whether pornography provided any benefit to women.

Regarding the first question, I appealed directly to women who were involved in the production of hard-core pornography such as S/M, where it seemed most likely that violence would occur. In the hundreds of such adult women I spoke with, every single one said they had not been coerced into performing pornography, nor did they know of a woman who had been. I decided to take the articulate voices of these adult women seriously and not dismiss them, as anti-porn feminists were doing.

To such evidence, radical feminists routinely answer that no "healthy" woman would consent to pornography. Therefore, such women were damaged by a male culture and incapable of rendering consent. The Minneapolis ordinance had argued that women, like children, needed special protection under the law: "Children are incapable of consenting to engage in pornographic conduct, even absent physical coercion, and therefore require special protection. By the same token, the physical and psychological well-being of women ought to be afforded comparable protection. . . ."

"A Woman's Body, a Woman's Right"

In the 19th century, women battled to become the legal equals of men, to have their consent taken seriously in the form of contracts and to have control of their own bodies legally recognized. Now anti-pornography feminists are asking the law to dismiss women's written consent.

Moreover, consider how contemptuously radical feminism is treating the "unacceptable" choices of these adult women. If a woman enjoys consuming pornography, it is not because she comes from another background, has a different psychological makeup, different goals in life or an unusual perspective. No: it is because she is mentally incompetent. Like any three-year-old, she is unable to give informed consent regarding her own body.

The touchstone principle of feminism used to be, "a woman's body, a woman's right." With regard to rape, radical feminists still declare, "No means no." But on some sexual matters, saying "yes" apparently means nothing. Pornography could not degrade women more than this attitude does.

As to whether cultural pressure has influenced the decisions of porn actresses—of course it has. Our culture has some impact on every choice we make, including the choice to become a feminist. To say that women who participate in pornography cannot make a choice because of cultural pressure, however, is to eliminate the possibility of choice in any situation.

What of women who do not become involved, who detest pornography? The simple answer is that they should not buy it. Moreover, they should use peaceful means to persuade others that pornography is improper. But they should not use the law.

Here, the second question initially posed comes into play: How does porn relate to general societal violence against women?

The radical feminist argument runs: Pornography leads directly to violence against women, especially rape. Thus, every woman is a victim because every woman is in danger.

This argument assumes:

That pornography impacts on people's behavior,

That the impact can be measured objectively and

That it can be related to sexual violence.

Pornography and Sexual Aggression

Pornography may well impact upon behavior, although recent studies question the extent. But it is extraordinarily difficult objectively to measure that impact. Sexual responses are extremely complex, and elude artificial lab conditions. Moreover, the standards used and the conclusions drawn usually depend on the bias of researchers and those who commission the research.

For example, in 1983, the Metropolitan Toronto Task Force on Violence Against Women commissioned Thelma McCormack to study pornography's connection to sexual aggression. McCormack's study indicated that pornography might be cathartic and, so, it might reduce the incidence of rape. Her report was discarded and reassigned to David Scott, a non-feminist committed to anti-pornography, who produced more palatable conclusions.

Statistics, Assumptions and Biases

Statistics almost always contain assumptions and biases. Sometimes the bias is an honest one. For example, a researcher who believes that sexual aggression is a learned behavior will naturally ask different questions than someone who believes aggression is an instinct. Other forms of bias are not so honest. For example, when a reporter for the Boston *Phoenix* asked the radical feminist Susan Brownmiller to supply some evidence for her assertions, she snapped back: "The statistics will come. We supply the ideology; it's for other people to come up with the statistics."

For the sake of argument, let's assume that a correlation exists between pornography and rape. What would such a correlation prove? A correlation is not a cause-and-effect relationship. It is a logical fallacy to assume that if A is correlated with B, then A causes B. Both might be caused by a totally separate factor, C. For example, there is a high correlation between the number of doctors in a city and the amount of alcohol consumed there. One does not cause the other. Both result from a third factor: the size of the city's population.

Censoring Pornography Does More Harm than Good

The evidence suggests that censorship of *any* material increases an audience's desire to obtain the material and disposes the audience to be more receptive to it. Critical viewing skills, and the ability to regard media images skeptically and analytically, atrophy under a censorial regime. A public that learns to question everything it sees or hears is better equipped to reject culturally propagated values than is one that assumes the media have been purged of all "incorrect" perspectives.

Even assuming for the sake of argument that there were a causal link between pornography and anti-female discrimination and violence, the insignificant contribution that censorship might make to reducing them would not outweigh the substantial damage that censorship would do to feminist goals. From the lack of actual evidence to substantiate the alleged causal link, the conclusion follows even more inescapably: *Censoring pornography would do women more harm than good.*

Nadine Strossen, *Defending Pornography: Free Speech, Sex, and the Fight for Women's Rights*, 1995.

Similarly, a correlation between pornography and rape may indicate nothing more than a common cause for both. Namely, that we live in a sexually-repressed society. To further repress sex by restricting pornography might well increase the incidence of rape. Opening up the area of pornography might well diffuse sexual violence by making sexuality more understandable.

State Oppression

There is great irony in radical feminists aligning with their two greatest ideological enemies: conservatives and the patriarchal state. They now appeal to this state as a protector. There is a sadness to the irony: it has been state regulation, not free speech, that has oppressed women. It was the state, not pornography, that burned women as witches. It was 18th-century law, not pornography, that defined women as chattel. 19th-century laws allowed men to commit wayward women to insane asylums, to claim their wives' earnings, and to beat them with impunity. Now 20th-century anti-porn laws may define what sexual choices are acceptable for women to make.

Benefits of Pornography

Indeed, pornography brings benefits to women. In censoring pornography, the state will impoverish rather than enrich them. Lisa Duggan explains: "The existence of pornography has served to flout conventional sexual mores, to ridicule sexual hypocrisy and to underscore the importance of sexual needs. Pornography carries many messages . . . it advocates sexual adventure, sex outside of marriage, sex for pleasure, casual sex, illegal sex, anonymous sex, public sex, voyeuristic sex. Some of these ideas appeal to women reading or seeing pornography, who may interpret some images as legitimating their own sense of sexual urgency or desire to be sexually aggressive."

Pornography and feminism have much in common. Both deal with women as valid sexual beings. They share a history of being targeted by obscenity laws, such as the Comstock laws (1870s) which were used against pornography and birth-control information. Feminist material—especially lesbian material—has always suffered under the regulation of sexual expression.

Sexual Liberation and Freedom of Speech

Two burning questions that confront women at the turn of the century are: Can feminism embrace sexual liberation? Can the freedom of women and freedom of speech remain fellow travelers?

The feminist Myra Kostash answers the latter by paraphrasing Camus: "Freedom to publish and read does not necessarily assure a society of justice and peace, but without these freedoms it has no assurance at all."

> "*The works most highly praised and rewarded by the self-seeking arts establishment always seem to trade in pornography, perversion . . . and the most grotesque forms of sensualism.*"

The National Endowment for the Arts Should Censor Pornographic Art

Center for Reclaiming America

The Center for Reclaiming America is an outreach of Coral Ridge Ministries, a religious institution whose goal is to reestablish traditional moral values in America. In the following viewpoint, the Center argues that art once celebrated the human spirit, but today, it degrades humanity with pornographic images and other assaults on traditional moral values. The Center contends that the National Endowment for the Arts (NEA)—a federal program that funds artists and art projects—should censor all obscene art.

As you read, consider the following questions:
1. What does Harold O.J. Brown argue is the function of art?
2. Why does the Center for Reclaiming America oppose Robert Mapplethorpe's art?
3. How can art become a weapon in the class struggle, according to Herbert Marcuse?

From chapter 15, The National Endowment for the Arts, of *Issues Tearing Our Nation's Fabric*, a publication of the Center for Reclaiming America; © Coral Ridge Ministries 2000. All rights reserved. Reprinted with permission.

M ost Americans hold a high view of art. We are amazed at the splendid lifelike sculptures of the Greeks and Romans; we delight in the magnificent music, paintings, and sculptures of the Renaissance; we are stirred by the probing insight and splendid detail of the Dutch Masters; and inspired by the imagination and joie de vivre [the celebration of life] of the Impressionists. We can appreciate the playful insolence of Pablo Picasso, Salvadore Dali, and Piet Mondrian, and also the edgy taunts of Claes Oldenburg, Jackson Pollock, Andy Warhol, and Roy Lichtenstein. But there is a point at which taste, like common sense, has its limits.

Art that inspires, challenges, and uplifts the soul has a rich history and deep significance in the American experience; but inspiring and uplifting art has been in very short supply the last fifty years. As if to reward and encourage the darkest and most destructive visions of modern life, the federal government, through massive funding of the National Endowment for the Arts (NEA), doles out millions of dollars every year to artists and institutions whose single-minded goal is apparently to assault the sensibilities of civilized people.

As if our tax dollars mean less than nothing, the NEA lavishes grants on artists and works whose only purpose is the debasement of life, the imagination, and the soul. Instead of celebrating the invincible human spirit or the majesty of creation, they wallow in anger and self-loathing. And the works most highly praised and rewarded by the self-seeking arts establishment always seem to trade in pornography, perversion, anti-American and anti-religious bigotry, and the most grotesque forms of sensualism and despair.

When funding time comes each year, the art community trots out its lists of grants to museums, civic theaters, symphonies, and touring exhibits that offer more wholesome fare. But as soon as the cameras are gone, and once the glare of public scrutiny is removed, the real work begins—which is the intentional, systematic, strategic, and meticulous grinding down of artistic sensibilities and public morality disguised under the name of art. All the outraged Hollywood celebrities the NEA can muster cannot hide that fact.

In his perceptive new book, *The Sensate Culture: Western Culture Between Chaos and Transformation*, Harold O.J. Brown says that art reflects the spirit of a nation and the spirit of the times. Think, for example, of Michelangelo's Italy, Thomas Gainsborough's England, or Vincent Van Gogh's Holland. And then consider how the twisted visions of Max Ernst and the "degenerate" artists of Nazi Germany reflected the chaos and spleen of the Third Reich. Art reflects the soul of the nation. Brown writes, "The spirit that pervades the arts and entertainment of the West today is shaping a culture of which only the degenerate can be proud." The consequence, he adds, is just as in economics: "Bad art, like bad money, drives out the good."

It is only natural, when the cultural elites make a habit of promoting, funding, and pushing upon society the darkest and most sordid visions of life, that the citizens should protest and rise up in alarm. It is to be expected, when elitist pronouncements about the deep and therapeutic "messages" of trashy works of art come into conflict with public decency and good taste, that the people paying the bills should expect and demand accountability. But when citizens demur, the arts establishment (flanked by its Hollywood contingent and the liberal media) cry censorship, repression, and intolerance, and accuse the responsible and respectable majority of muzzling their "freedom of expression."

But while the political, cultural, intellectual, and media elites demand unlimited freedom of expression, they are the very first to silence any public expression of religion. While they want the world to applaud homoerotic displays, fetishism, flag-burning, naked dancing, empty canvases, empty stages, empty minds, or live sex acts on stage, they cannot abide the simple decency, honor, and family values that cherish natural expressions of affection and the bond of mother, father, and child. Modesty, decency, self-respect, and discretion have no place in that worldview.

Appeals by those who are shocked and offended by the outrages of the arts league are ignored unless somehow it affects funding. "In the present climate of 'anything goes,'" writes Harold Brown:

> There is little chance to suppress art that is obscene, pornographic, cruel, and depraved. Instead, suppression is aimed at things that were formerly considered edifying, touching, and

uplifting, such as religious symbols, affirmations of faith, references to God or salvation. The Ten Commandments, which once were taken for granted as the foundation of public law and justice in the United States, have been removed from schoolrooms and courtrooms. The tendencies to censorship are not limited to religious matters. Portrayals of noble or self-sacrificing figures, wholesome role models, and romantic or sentimental figures from history and legend are prohibited or, if permitted, are shown only in distorted and dishonoring forms.

The Record Speaks

When citizens protested arts funding in the early 1990s, the New York media flooded the news with cries of outrage from the luminaries of stage, screen, and the arts. They did not, however, show the works of Andres Serrano and Robert Mapplethorpe that created the controversy. ABC showed Mapplethorpe's flower photos and spoke warmly of his struggle against "homophobia" and intolerance.

They did not show the works of "art" our tax dollars supported featuring frontal male nudity, human waste, Mapplethorpe's photo of a bullwhip protruding from his own

anus, or a homosexual man urinating into another man's mouth. They did not show Serrano's photograph of a crucifix in a jar of the artist's urine, with the title "Piss Christ." Later, art critic Lucy Lippard, writing in *Art in America*, called Serrano's photo, "darkly beautiful." But that's not how America saw it.

"If this is art," one lawmaker protested, "then why not sell it on the open market? The free market is the best proving ground for new ideas. If this is of such value that the NEA will fund it, then why settle for tax dollars? You can go public." But such common-sense reactions inflamed artistic sensibilities. In response, the *New York Times* ran a two-page feature story on four artists whose grant requests were rejected after the flap in 1990. These "artists" do not paint, write, or sculpt; they rail against society. One of the four, a female, spews four-letter words and vulgar curses while smearing herself with human excrement. The others are homosexuals who scream about the sin of "homophobia." One of them, John Fleck, told reporters, "I became known as the man who masturbated on stage and urinated on the Bible."

Playwright Holly Hughes said, "My work has always been about publicly representing or revealing a lesbian experience. . . . to become visible, to leave the ghetto, to not be marginalized." After the Clinton Administration restored NEA funding, Hughes received not only an official apology but four more grants for new works, including one for her play, "The Well of Horniness," which celebrates lesbian sexuality and masturbation.

Over the last three years, under a more conservative majority in Congress, public funding for the arts has dropped from $170 million to $99 million per year, and many are lobbying aggressively for total defunding of the NEA. The reasons should be clear. Thomas Jefferson said that requiring citizens to support with their own money ideas with which they disagree is "sinful and tyrannical." The arts endowment would like Americans to believe they stand for art and culture, when their record shows conclusively what they really stand for: depravity, deception, and intellectual tyranny.

One has to wonder where the destructive perspectives of the NEA and the elites come from. How can any sane or rational mind believe that the total annihilation of art in the name of free expression can be good for civilization? At least part of the answer has to come from the sources that schooled the minds of the men and women who administer cultural establishments today. It helps to remember that those in authority in the arts world are, by and large, products of the 1960s.

Do No Harm

Congress thus concluded that . . . the National Endowment for the Arts (NEA) should desist from funding celebrations of depravity or insults, borrowing from the Hippocratic Oath: first, do no harm. Thus, Congress amended the NEA charter to require the chairman to consider "general standards of decency and respect for the diverse beliefs and values of the American public" in assessing the artistic merit of a grant application. It left undisturbed, however, the substance and spirit of French poet Voltaire's salute to freedom of speech: "I disapprove of what you say, but I will defend to death your right to say it." The "decency and respect" amendment placed no limits or penalties on artistic expression funded by a modern benefactor . . . or private institutions or without remuneration.

Bruce Fein, *Washington Times*, November 19, 1996.

One of those influences was the German social philosopher and college professor, Herbert Marcuse, who came to this country in the 1930s. A radical Marxist devoted to the overthrow of capitalism, Marcuse wrote revolutionary tracts, thinly disguised as philosophy, encouraging American youth to reject their democratic heritage and moral values he called "repressive and conformist." His books, *Eros and Civilization*, *One-Dimensional Man*, and *The Aesthetic Dimension*, became textbooks for revolution in the hands of Leftists. And Marcuse found an army of willing soldiers in the universities.

"Art can indeed become a weapon in the class struggle," Marcuse taught, "by promoting changes in the prevailing consciousness." But first, painting, sculpture, theater, and music had to be stripped of conventional values.

While, in the arts, in literature and music, in communication, in the mores and fashions, changes have occurred which suggest a new experience, a radical transformation of values, the social structure and its political expressions seem to remain basically unchanged, or at least lagging behind the cultural revolution.

However, by the time of his death in 1979, all those things were under attack.

In his analysis of the moral breakdown in American society, E. Michael Jones frames the central issue extremely well:

A mind clouded by passion is like a window covered with dirt. It is not transparent; it is aware only of itself. Virtually all the artistic breakthroughs of the modern age . . . are a function of the mind turned away from truth and focused on its own desires instead. The turning away from the truth at the behest of disordered passions does not mean that the mind will stop functioning; it only means that that mind will not perceive the truth. And after a period of laboring in the dark, the mind can choose disorder over order and create for itself idols that it will serve instead of the truth placed in the universe by the Creator who is synonymous with truth.

Restoring the Moral Order

Given thirty years to foment and resonate within the universities, the arts community, the cultural establishment, and the coffee houses of New York City and San Francisco these fatuous and self-centered nostrums of the sixties reappear in our time, fully fledged as a revolutionary movement now taking its legitimacy from the NEA, the federal government, and your tax dollars.

The apostle Paul said,

whatever things are true, whatever things are noble, whatever things are just, whatever things are pure, whatever things are lovely, whatever things are of good report, if there is any virtue and if there is anything praiseworthy; meditate on these things.

For centuries the vision of great art has been the ennobling of the mind, the building of character and perceptions, and a celebration of the world as God made it. How tragic that we could have come so far from that view.

"[Democratic societies should give] support to legitimate visionary artists, no matter how offensive their works may seem to certain organized coalitions."

The National Endowment for the Arts Should Not Censor Pornographic Art

Robert Brustein

Robert Brustein maintains in the following viewpoint that the National Endowment for the Arts (NEA)—a federal program that funds artists and art projects—should not censor art which the majority deems pornographic. Basing artistic merit on the majority's sense of decency, Brustein asserts, silences minority opinions. Brustein contends that original and imaginative works of art challenge and educate the electorate and make democracy possible. Robert Brustein is a staff writer for the *New Republic*, a weekly magazine.

As you read, consider the following questions:
1. According to Brustein, what book by James Joyce was banned from the United States because it violated "community standards"?
2. In Brustein's opinion, why is the word "obscene" difficult to define?
3. Why must the government continue to support the serious arts, according to the author?

Reprinted from Robert Brustein, "Sex, Art, and the Supreme Court," *The New Republic*, October 5, 1998, by permission of *The New Republic*; © 1998, The New Republic, Inc.

H istory will take a while to demonstrate the folly of the Supreme Court's 1998 eight-to-one decision upholding the decency test in awarding arts grants through the National Endowment for the Arts (NEA).

That particular Representative Jesse Helms–sponsored clause, you may remember, commanded the NEA to take into account what it called "general standards of decency and respect for the diverse beliefs and values of the American public" when disbursing money to artists and arts groups. Some concurring justices, believing the 1990 law contained only "advisory language," excused their decision by saying that the clause was essentially "toothless" anyway. Sandra Day O'Connor, for example, declared that the statute would violate the First Amendment if it actually imposed "a penalty on disfavored viewpoints." In other words, you can always appeal to the legal system if you feel your right to speech has been infringed. But if this is so, then why not get rid of the damned thing altogether instead of having to resort to litigation every time the statute is imposed?

Other justices, I believe, read the future more accurately. Disputing O'Connor's sanguine interpretation, Antonin Scalia said that he would consider even an outright ban on federal financing of indecent art to be constitutional. Clarence Thomas agreed. Only Justice David H. Souter recognized that such a statute, however interpreted or administered, was a form of content restriction, hence a clear instance of viewpoint discrimination, and should have been struck down.

None of the justices brought up the really vexing question, which is how it ever came to be assumed that the public at large has the right to decide on morality in the arts. The whole notion of "general standards of decency and respect," otherwise known as "community standards," has never been intelligently debated in this country, though this dubious concept has been eloquently denounced by many thinkers, among them Mill, Nietzsche, Ibsen, Shaw, Santayana, Unamuno, and Mencken. It was "community standards" that for years banned works by D.H. Lawrence, Henry Miller, and, most notably, James Joyce, whose *Ulysses* took more than ten years to get published in the United States. In a landmark decision in 1933, John M. Woolsey, a United States District Judge, ruled that while "somewhat emetic, nowhere does [*Ulysses*] tend to be an aphrodisiac." He concluded that the book was therefore not obscene in the legal definition of the word, namely as "tending to stir the sex impulses or lead to sexually impure and lustful thoughts."

So, Americans finally got the chance to ingest the emetic *Ulysses* as a literary supplement to milk of magnesia. But such a definition would have technically prevented us from openly buying erotic books by such authors as Rabelais, Aretino, or Boccaccio, among others more erotic than cathartic. In his classic essay "Pornography and Obscenity," Lawrence ridiculed a British home secretary who harbored a similar definition of obscenity. Outraged over some improper literature, that official had bellowed: "And these two young people, who had been perfectly pure up till that time, after reading this book went out and had sexual intercourse together!!!"—to which Lawrence jubilantly retorted: "One up to them!" Lawrence was hardly a proselytizer for promiscuity. He probably conformed to a stricter moral code than any of his detractors (holding the curious opinion, for example, that masturbation was "the most dangerous sexual vice that society can be afflicted with"). But Lawrence also knew that behind the rabid fulminations of the Comstocks and the Grundys and the Bowdlers [famous censors] lurked a true obscenity, and perhaps the raison d'être [reason for being] of pornography, namely "the grey disease of sex hatred," the desire to keep sex "a dirty little secret." (To him, the emancipated bohemians were not a whole lot better since, in killing off the dirty little secret through public promiscuity and group sex, they also managed to kill off whatever was dark and private in the erotic life.)

Lawrence was even more passionate on the subject of "community standards." First of all, how does a community decide an issue of "obscenity" when no one knows what the term means? Supposedly derived from the Latin *obscena*, meaning that which might not be represented on the stage, it is a word originally driven by the traditional Puritan hostility toward the theater as a form. Since not all of us are Puritans, how then can we arrive at a single community standard? "What is obscene to Tom is not obscene to Lucy or Joe," Lawrence wrote, "and really, the meaning of a word has to wait for majorities to decide it." Majorities, majorities. Only what poet and essayist William Butler Yeats called "the mad intellect of democracy" could ever have devised the caprice that the mass of people corner wisdom in this matter. "We have to leave everything to the majority," Lawrence stormed, "everything to the majority, everything to the mob, the mob, the mob. . . . If the lower ten million doesn't know better than the upper ten men, then there's something wrong with mathematics. Take a vote on it. Show hands, and prove my count.". . .

The talented ten to whom Lawrence alluded have been almost universally scornful of this populist voice of God. Shakespeare had little respect for "the many-headed multitude." Mill castigated "the tyranny of the majority." Ibsen was certain "the majority is always wrong." Shaw joked that "forty million Frenchmen can't be right." Mencken inveighed against "boobocracy." In response to which contemporary populists and majoritarians everywhere would undoubtedly unleash their favorite epithet: "elitists."

But like most of the other thinkers, Lawrence had the capacity to distinguish between what he called the "mobself," which mindlessly acquiesces in conventional opinions, and the "individual-self," which is capable of original, subtle, and imaginative thought. People have always longed for an informed electorate. The concept of an enlightened majority has been an elusive ideal ever since the invention of democracy. The most obvious way to achieve this has been through widespread dissemination of works of intellect and the arts. But instead of absorbing the best that has been thought and created in any age, the mass of people in modern industrial societies is invariably bombarded with the most debased forms of opinion and entertainment—being manipulated, diddled, and scammed by those who will use any available means of communication to expand their own powers. It was Lawrence who observed that "the public, which is feeble-minded like an idiot, will never be able to preserve its individual reactions from the tricks of the exploiter." Indeed, the ideal of an enlightened majority grows more and more distant as our advanced technology gets more and more skillful at influencing minds. Today, the religious right, among other influential groups, is using the media to blitz us with all manner of anxieties, hypocrisies, mind gropes, fears, and lies. Americans no longer turn for wisdom to Emerson or Dewey, but to evangelist Jerry Falwell and presidential hopeful Pat Robertson, if not to media hosts Rush Limbaugh, Geraldo Rivera, and Don Imus.

The Marketplace of Ideas

All aspects of our culture, including the arts, influence our attitudes and ideas about the world. Art, music, advertising, the mass media, education, religious training, families and communities, all shape the kind of people we are. Each "bad" idea competes with all other ideas an individual encounters in the media, and from life's most effective teacher: real world experience. A person who learned respect for others early on will not be converted to hooliganism by the movies. Moreover, human beings are various and idiosyncratic; we each respond to art, literature, and pop culture in different ways. The value of free speech is that it permits a wide range of ideas to flourish so that individuals can grow, learn and decide for themselves what ideas to accept or reject.

Feminists for Free Expression, www.well.com/user/freedom, 1999.

The question that remains, however, is federal funding for the arts, and why the public should be required to pay for something that offends the religious or moral sensibilities of some of its members. It is a difficult question to argue without also explaining why the public should pay for something that doesn't interest the great majority—classical music, for example, or modern dance. As economist John Kenneth Galbraith never tires of reminding us, even in a capitalist society the government is responsible for a number of services not determined by the market—the police department, the fire department, public housing, health, sanitation, education, the courts, government itself. Even a galloping market economy has the capacity to recognize that certain crucial needs are not adequately supplied through competition, and chief among these are the serious arts. Do we need to be told again that the greatest books of any time rarely make the bestseller lists, that the finest works of music are hardly to be found on the pop charts, that the best plays are seldom the biggest box-office bonanzas? Let the market drive the popular arts—Hollywood, Broadway, Madison Avenue, and Motown. The serious arts cannot survive without patronage and support.

But what right has government to assess my precious tax dollars if I am not a patron of the opera or a visitor to museums? Put aside the fact that with the present appropriation to the NEA (less than $100 million annually, much of it going to State Arts Councils), I am not even contributing tax dollars, or even a tax dollar, or even half a dollar to the arts, but a figure closer to thirty cents, why should I be required to contribute a penny if there's no immediate benefit?

I don't believe that this is a serious question. If it were, then why wasn't I consulted when being assessed infinitely larger amounts for such inestimable boons to humankind as the Vietnam War [which the United States lost], the B-1 bomber [that became too expensive and obsolete to build], or the Strategic Defense Initiative [that was proven technologically infeasible]? It is only when contemplating subsidies to the arts and the humanities that the public is supposed to have a deciding voice. And even then that voice is not respected or heeded: recent polls assure us that most Americans still favor larger Federal subsidies for the arts.

The nub of the matter remains obscenity and impiety. Should I be obliged to contribute even thirty cents to look at photographs of Robert Mapplethorpe with a whip handle up his butt or be affronted by Andres Serrano's urinedipped crucifix or watch Karen Finley smear her naked body with chocolate syrup? The answer is: I can always turn my face away. One of the blessings of a democracy is freedom of choice. I have the freedom to choose among the countless other works of art available to me, or not to look at anything. The Finley show, the Mapplethorpe photographs and Serrano photographs are only three among thousands of undisputed artworks that have been partially supported by federal subsidy, and no one is requiring me to patronize them.

If I did, however, I might discover that Finley's infamous chocolate act was less designed for prurient display than for making some statement about the female body, just as Andres Serrano's notorious photograph was trying to tell us something about the commercial exploitation of religious objects. I confess I don't see much value in Mapplethorpe's X portfolio, but nothing compels me to look at it. The problem is sectarian sensitivities. In an atmosphere of delicate, easily wounded feelings—an atmosphere to which the politically correct left has certainly contributed a fair share of moans and groans—such expressions were bound to outrage certain factions. Still, it is useful to remember that, in addition to guaranteeing the rights of the majority, our form of government is also dedicated to guaranteeing the rights of dissenting opinion so long as it doesn't incite violence. It is a fact of history that the vanguard has rarely been able to collect a majority for its ideas or creations until years after the advances have been absorbed by the establishment.

It is the obligation of a democratic society, however, to protect the magical idea from those who would politicize it into a program or a slogan. And that means, of course, giving support to legitimate visionary artists, no matter how offensive their works may seem to certain organized coalitions. It may not be the primary purpose of the arts to provoke the populace, but this function is often the consequence of any artistic expression attempting to break new ground. American civilization, like all societies, exists not only in the present but in the future as well. We remember Athens less for the Peloponnesian Wars than for Aeschylus, Sophocles, Euripides, Sappho, Plato, and Aristotle. We value the Elizabethans not so much for overcoming the Spanish Armada as for producing the works of Spenser, Marlowe, Shakespeare, and Jonson. We admire Victorian England not for colonizing half the globe, but for bringing forth the novels of Dickens, Thackeray, and George Eliot. Do Americans wish to be remembered primarily for gangsta rap, the T.V. show *Seinfeld*, the musical *Rent*, and the movie *Titanic*? All those attempting to help mold the American future through creative expression, all those who care about how our presentday society will be perceived by posterity, can only be dismayed and appalled by this Supreme Court decision.

Periodical Bibliography

The following articles have been selected to supplement the diverse views presented in this chapter. Addresses are provided for periodicals not indexed in the *Readers' Guide to Periodical Literature*, the *Alternative Press Index*, the *Social Sciences Index*, or the *Index to Legal Periodicals and Books*.

Amy Adler	"Photography on Trial," *Index on Censorship*, May/June 1996.
Walter Berns	"Pornography Versus Democracy," *Society*, September/October 1999.
Nina Burleigh	"The Pornographers," *Arete*, March/April 1989.
Karen Finley	"The Art of Offending," *The New York Times*, November 14, 1996.
Bruce Handy	"Beyond the Pale," *Time*, March 16, 1998.
Irving Kristol	"Liberal Censorship and the Common Culture," *Society*, September/October 1999.
John Leo	"Hold the Chocolate," *U.S. News & World Report*, July 13, 1998.
Nation	"Cynthia Stewart's Ordeal," May 1, 2000.
Marcia Pally	"'Decency in the Arts,'" *Tikkun*, November/December 1998.
Garrett Peck	"The Censor as Unwitting Ally," *Gauntlet*, 1998. Available from Dept. 98A, 309 Powell Rd., Springfield, PA 19064.
Rachel A. Roemhildt	"Americans Wouldn't Know It, but Pornography Is Illegal," *Insight*, December 14, 1998. Available from 3600 New York Ave. NE, Washington, DC 20002.
Dennis Saffran	"Pinups for Pedophiles, the Latest Legal Right," *Wall Street Journal*, July 22, 1998.
Nadine Strossen	"The Perils of Pornophobia," *Humanist*, May/June 1995.
George Will	"The Art of Funding," *Newsweek*, July 6, 1998.

CHAPTER 3

How Should Internet Pornography Be Regulated?

Chapter Preface

In the past, store clerks tried to make sure that children did not look at or buy the pornographic magazines on their store's shelves. Indeed, pornography was difficult to obtain, and young people had to search hard to find it. But today, a child can access scores of pornographic images in the comfort of his or her own bedroom with a few clicks of a mouse.

The Internet has been largely unregulated, with the exception of one attempt in 1996 to stop the proliferation of pornography in cyberspace. A portion of the Telecommunications Act of 1996, called the Communications Decency Act (CDA), made it illegal to disseminate "indecent" material over the Internet. Supporters of the CDA contended that it was important to crack down on cyberporn in order to protect children, who increasingly have unlimited access to computers and the Internet. Nebraska senator Jim Exon, who sponsored the Senate version of the bill, argued that the CDA merely applied current obscenity laws to computers and was therefore not unconstitutional. He asserted that the CDA "could help to ensure that our kids have a chance to travel safely through cyberspace."

Many civil libertarians, online service companies and others protested that the CDA was unconstitutional, however. When the CDA passed, Ira Glasser, executive director of the American Civil Liberties Union, argued, "Nothing less than the future of free expression in the United States is at stake here." Many opponents of the CDA argued that the Internet was a unique, decentralized medium that offered unheard of opportunities for open communication and should stay that way. In 1997 the Supreme Court struck down the law, ruling that it was too vaguely worded and would result in the suppression of adult speech.

The passage and subsequent striking down of the Communications Decency Act illustrates how difficult it is to protect minors from harm while not infringing on the public's constitutional right to free speech. The authors in the following chapter debate how society should respond to pornography on the Internet.

"I have yet to hear a decent argument from any so-called 'free speech' advocates on why pornographers should be free to peddle their material to children via computers."

The Government Should Censor Internet Pornography

Maryam Kubasek

Maryam Kubasek is director of communications at the Cincinnati-based National Coalition for the Protection of Children & Families. In the following viewpoint, she argues that the constitutional protection of free speech does not apply to pornography on the Internet. Children have always been protected from pornography, Kubasek maintains, because pornography is violent and degrading. Therefore, she contends that laws should be enacted to stop pornographic materials from being transmitted through cyberspace.

As you read, consider the following questions:
1. What protective measures does Kubasek recommend for protecting children from Internet pornography?
2. According to the author, what types of pornography are available on the Internet?
3. In what other venues have children been denied access to pornography, according to Kubasek?

Reprinted, with permission, from Maryam Kubasek, "Limit Access to Pornography," *The Christian Science Monitor*, February 29, 1996.

W ould the folks out there who think it's perfectly acceptable to hand a child a pornographic magazine please step forward?

Free Speech Advocates Are Wrong

I have yet to hear a decent argument from any so-called "free speech" advocates on why pornographers should be free to peddle their material to children via computers. Because that's what all the rhetoric about the Communications Decency Amendment of the Telecommunications Reform Bill boils down to.[1] Congress decided it should be illegal to knowingly transmit or display pornography to kids.

It's that simple. Incorporate passwords, genuine age-verification, and other protective measures for the sort of material we have never given children access to. The Internet was designed to withstand a nuclear attack. Don't tell me the clever minds that make this technological world turn can't find a way to keep a 12-year-old from accessing pictures of women and children being degraded or abused.

But the American Civil Liberties Union (ACLU) avoids that discussion, instead favoring claims that literary masterpieces and important health discussions are in jeopardy.[2] Perhaps, like Chicken Little, they've screamed that the sky is falling once too often. They don't want people to know that types of pictorial/image pornography available on the Internet include everything from soft-core newsstand porn to hard-core sex acts, including bestiality, torture of women for sexual pleasure, and other acts of the most degrading kind, as well as child pornography. Types of textual pornography include detailed stories on the rape, mutilation, and torture of women; sexual abuse of children; and incest.

The Law Must Protect Children

Yes, heaven forbid that a child—or anyone else for that matter—shouldn't have easy access to such photos. Let's just put the onus for keeping kids away from this garbage on par-

1. The Communications Decency Amendment was ruled unconstitutional by the Supreme Court in 1997.   2. The ACLU filed suit against the government, claiming that the Communications Decency Amendment was unconstitutional. The ACLU won its suit in 1997.

ents instead of on the producers and distributors. At all costs, we're told, we should avoid creating any legal liability for the pornographers and just trust them to be good citizens. We don't give kids access to pornography in bookstores, video stores, or dial-a-porn. It would be ridiculous and irresponsible. But the ACLU and others are suggesting that should be different in cyberspace.

Decency Laws Are Deterrents

Opponents [of laws that would censor the Internet] forsake reason when they say they want to protect children from indecency, seduction and harassment but maintain that the overriding issue is freedom of access to anything by anybody. Tell that to a parent who has had a child lured away by a deviant on a computer network. Hardly a day goes by without another story about the mix of depravity and children on the 'net. How many more are never reported?

We have laws against murder, and we have laws against speeding. We still have murder, and we still have speeding. But I think most reasonable people would agree that we very likely would have more murders and more speeders if we didn't have laws as deterrents.

Decency laws won't make the Internet pristine, but it will help protect our children.

Jim Exon, *ComputerWorld*, February 19, 1996.

The next generation, for whom this technology offers the most promise, should be as welcome on the Internet as adults. Women should be as welcome as men. Adults who are interested in this material have access to hundreds of other sites for computer pornography (private commercial pornographic bulletin board services), where it is possible to check subscribers' ages.

Our society has a historic commitment to protecting children from the worst impulses of adults. And most who are in favor of protective measures aren't fanatics—religious, cultural, or otherwise. They're just reasonable people who don't think it's a good idea to allow children into a world of dangerous material for which they are not psychologically prepared.

Most people don't trust the pornography industry's "goodwill" to stay away from kids unless they face laws telling them they must. The fanaticism is to be found in the ranks of those who contend that on the Internet, anything goes, and no material is too explicit or too violent or too degrading. This shift in the baseline for children's access to pornography is remarkably callous; it would mark a fundamental change in our historic attitude toward the law's role in helping protect kids.

The ACLU and others need to quit hiding behind "free speech" rhetoric and at least have the intellectual honesty to tell the truth. They're cheapening the legitimate free-speech argument by using it to defend distribution of pornography to children.

"It is indeed possible . . . for minors to get access to raunchy fare on the Internet . . . but that is no mandate for a federal criminal law."

The Government Should Not Censor Internet Pornography

Stephen Chapman

Stephen Chapman contends in the following viewpoint that enacting laws against transmitting pornography over the Internet infringes on the constitutional right to free speech. Chapman admits that children can access pornography via the Internet, but he points out that they can also get pornography in bookstores and video stores. He argues that parental supervision and other voluntary actions that have worked to protect children from pornography in more traditional venues can also protect children from Internet pornography. Stephen Chapman is a syndicated columnist.

As you read, consider the following questions:

1. In Chapman's opinion, why are people more concerned about pornography on the Internet than pornography found in traditional print media?
2. According to the author, why did three federal judges overturn the Communications Decency Act?
3. What can happen to content providers who fail to block minors' access to Internet pornography, according to Chapman?

Reprinted from Stephen Chapman, "Foiling an Attack on Free Expression," syndicated column of July 3, 1996, by permission of Stephen Chapman and Creators Syndicate, Inc.

I f aspirin were invented today, it has been said, the Food and Drug Administration would not allow it on the market because the drug is not entirely free of risk. By the same token, we can be grateful that ink and paper didn't make their first appearance the day before yesterday. Otherwise, Congress and the president would be scrambling frantically to make sure that these communication tools would not be used for purposes unapproved by the government.

A free press is generally taken for granted when it comes to the realm of printed words and pictures. Being familiar with the medium, and occasionally bored with it, we aren't terrified by the possibility that it will be used in ways we don't particularly like. Incendiary political leaflets, racist books, pornographic magazines, Robert Mapplethorpe photos [depicting graphic homosexual sex acts]—most of us accept them all as part of a free and open society.

Fear of Technology

But let human ingenuity create new ways to deliver the same old words and images, and many Americans suddenly act as though they had never heard of the concept of free speech. An exaggerated regard for the power of technology overwhelms our experience, our good sense and our best principles.

That's how we got the Communications Decency Act of 1996 (CDA), which a Republican Congress and a Democratic president enacted in the full knowledge that it was almost certainly unconstitutional. In June 1996, a panel of three federal judges gave the law the fate it deserved, finding that it violated the First Amendment by interfering with the right of adults to choose what to read and see.[1] The surprise is not that the law was struck down but that anyone ever imagined it would be upheld.

The measure was supposed to stem the tide of sexually oriented material available on the vast computer network known as the Internet. Sen. James Exon (D-Neb.), the main sponsor, said it was needed to "keep the information highway from becoming a red-light district."

1. The June 1996 decision by the three judge panel was appealed, and the Communications Decency Act was sent to the Supreme Court. In 1997, the Supreme Court ruled that the CDA was unconstitutional.

Under the law, it is illegal to make certain material available to anyone under 18. It outlawed not only hard-core obscenity—which, by the Supreme Court's tortured reasoning, has no constitutional protection—but also anything merely "indecent," which could encompass anything from *Playboy* magazine to commonplace vulgar expressions to discussions of AIDS prevention to great works of art and literature.

A Key Ritual of Adolescence

Whatever control measures Congress can cook up for the Internet will be half-assed and ineffective, and any teen Web surfer worth her salt will find the filth without much difficulty. The hunt for porn—in whatever medium it presents itself—is a key ritual of adolescence, just as the attempt to hide all frank discussion of sexuality from adolescents is a key ritual of bourgeois adulthood.

Andrew O'Hehir, *Spin*, July 1997.

Since people who transmit material over the Internet— "content providers," as they are lovingly known—can't reliably block access to minors without going to great trouble and expense, they are potentially liable for any material they offer. If something sent out is deemed by a prosecutor and a jury to fall within the spacious and poorly marked boundaries of "indecency," the provider can be convicted of a felony, sent to prison and relieved of as much as a quarter of a million dollars.

Better Alternatives to Censorship

Now, it is indeed possible (though not terribly easy) for minors to get access to raunchy fare on the Internet—if they have a computer, a modem, some technical skills and inattentive parents. But that is no mandate for a federal criminal law.

After all, it is also possible (and a good deal cheaper and easier) for minors to get their hands on raunchy magazines, X-rated videos and Jackie Collins romance novels. But we manage to cope with that danger through a combination of voluntary action by stores and vigilance by parents. Similar efforts—including the use of various devices to let parents restrict their kids' access to the Internet—promise to let us cope equally well or better with the hazards posed by computer communications.

But we sometimes develop an irrational terror of any medium we haven't seen before—as if it has the magical power to take control of our minds. That fear is responsible for much of the federal regulation of broadcasting, which has never enjoyed the same constitutional guarantees as newspapers and books. It was also responsible for a 1988 federal law banning commercial "dial-a-porn" phone services.

The alleged goal was to protect children, almost all of whom can use a phone. But a unanimous Supreme Court threw out the law because it had, in the words of Justice Byron White, "the invalid effect of limiting the content of adult telephone conversations to that which is suitable for children to hear." Any politician who was paying the slightest attention could have figured out that the same defect would bring down the Communications Decency Act, as it did in June 1996.

Our elected officials in Washington think freedom should be confined to its traditional arenas, with the federal government exercising strict control over anything new and different. The judges who struck down the Internet law understood that freedom is indivisible.

"Software solutions [to block children from seeing pornography] are in relatively early stages of development. But they are already effective and affordable."

Filtering Software Can Limit Children's Access to Internet Pornography

Solveig Bernstein

In the following viewpoint, Solveig Bernstein contends that parents who are concerned about their children viewing pornography on the Internet can install filtering software on their home computers. Filtering software blocks out websites that contain pornography and can prevent children from performing searches that might locate unrated sites. Bernstein argues that laws regulating pornography on the Internet assume responsibility for protecting children—a responsibility that rightly belongs to parents. Solveig Bernstein is assistant director of telecommunications and technology studies at the Cato Institute, a libertarian public policy research foundation.

As you read, consider the following questions:
1. In addition to using filtering software, what other solutions does Bernstein suggest to limit what children see on the Internet?
2. According to Bernstein, what is the difference between software that takes an "exclusive approach" and software that takes an "inclusive approach?"
3. In the author's opinion, what tactics might children use to try to evade filtering software controls?

Reprinted, with permission, from Solveig Bernstein, "Beyond the Communications Decency Act: Constitutional Lessons of the Internet," *Cato Policy Analysis*, November 4, 1996.

The Supreme Court has described the government's interest in regulating indecency as an interest in helping parents supervise their children—not in protecting children from indecency when their parents believe the materials in question would do their children no harm.

Law Should Not Replace Parents

Constitutional interpretation has consistently recognized that the parents' claim to authority in their own household to direct the rearing of their children is basic in the structure of our society. . . . The legislature could properly conclude that parents and others, teachers for example, who have this primary responsibility for children's well-being are entitled to the support of laws designed to aid discharge of that responsibility. . . .

It is not rational to argue, however, that government can have a compelling interest in helping concerned parents when concerned parents do not need help.

Filtering Software: A Private Solution

Government should not be able to argue that it has a compelling solution to a problem that has effective private solutions. Computer networks offer an excellent private solution to parents who want to protect their children from indecency, but who do not want to deny access to online services altogether. As with any media, parents can control their child's access to computerized indecency by exercising a little sense. Some parents, for example, do not allow their children access to online services in the privacy of their own rooms; access is available only by means of a computer in the family room, where anyone walking by can see what is on the screen. Technology is available to supplement parental supervision. Software is available to parents who want to restrict their children's access to indecent material online. The cost of filtering software is about $30 to $50—about the cost of a computer game, and not nearly as much as the computer itself.

An Exclusive Approach

Some filters block sites identified as undesirable (the "exclusive" approach). If such software operated only by blocking lists of sites actually visited and rated "bad," it would allow all unrated sites through. Thus, products such as CyberSitter, CyberPatrol, and SurfWatch also restrict the type of Web searches that a child can perform and restrict visits to unrated content by watching for words and phrases typical of sexually explicit material. One government witness during the Communications Decency Act (CDA) trial testified that he had been able to find sites that SurfWatch did not block. But he admitted during cross-examination that SurfWatch had been turned off during the searches he used to find those sites, and that SurfWatch would not have allowed him to perform those searches.

Filtering Software More Effective than Regulation

Filtering software installed on individual computers is more likely to be effective than blanket government regulations. . . .

These programs identify Web sites that contain potentially objectionable material and then block the computer from accessing them.

Karen Kaplan, *Los Angeles Times*, June 27, 1997.

Developers of filters that take the exclusive approach defend it on the grounds that undesirable sites are rare. Nigel Spicer, president of Microsystems, Inc., explains that "it's more effective to monitor the 1 percent of sites that are inappropriate."

An Inclusive Approach

Other software avoids the problem of unrated sites by allowing access only to rated sites (the "inclusive" approach). For example, users of CyberPatrol may opt to allow access only to the "CyberYES" list, which contains about 10,000 sites. SafeSurf, a voluntary rating organization, includes 50,000 child-friendly sites in its Cyber-Playground.

These software solutions are in relatively early stages of development. But they are already effective and affordable. As the technology advances, they will become even more so. Children might attempt to evade the controls, for example, by booting the computer from a floppy diskette and attempting to access the Internet directly without triggering the filtering software. Or a child might attempt to defeat the software by deleting files from config.sys. Gordon Ross explains that Net Nanny works at the operating systems level, monitoring the status of all files on the system. If a child attempts to use either evasion method, Net Nanny can shut down the computer or simply notify parents of the evasion attempts. CyberSitter has similar features. CyberPatrol prevents children from accessing the Internet after booting the computer from a floppy by monitoring all activity at the computer's communications port, and also shuts down the system in response to attempts to disable CyberPatrol's files, which upon installation are hidden throughout the operating system. Some devices, such as CyberSitter, also have the ability to report to parents which sites the child has visited. . . .

There are substantial reasons to believe that protecting children from a danger that the children's parents do not recognize as particularly grave should not amount to a compelling interest. As pointed out above, filtering software is affordable to anyone who can afford a computer system. Nonsupervising parents have implicitly decided that exposure to material of a sexual nature probably will not harm their children enough to bother with. If the parents do not find the interest sufficiently compelling to take action, there is no reason to think that government should.

"[The filtering software] Cybersitter is actually an extension of [the right-wing organization] Focus on the Family's antifeminist, antigay, anti-abortion rights agenda."

Parents Should Not Use Internet Filtering Software

Langdon Winner

Langdon Winner is director of graduate studies in the Department of Science and Technology Studies at Rensselaer Polytechnic Institute. In the following viewpoint, he argues that parents should resist installing filtering software that claims to protect their children from pornography on the Internet. He contends that such software often blocks legitimate, non-pornographic websites belonging to groups whose agenda the manufacturer disagrees with. Winner asserts that filtering software often pushes repressive social agendas and limits free speech.

As you read, consider the following questions:
1. What would be the purpose of a C-chip, according to Winner?
2. According to the author, what non-pornographic websites does CyberPatrol block?
3. Why does filtering software remind Winner of the totalitarian states early in the nineteenth century?

Reprinted from Langdon Winner, "Electronically Implanted 'Values,'" *Technology Review*, February/March 1997, by permission of *Technology Review*, via the Copyright Clearance Center.

Laws, regulations, police, education, propaganda—these are among the means societies have traditionally employed to promote and defend the values they deem crucial. Yet these efforts are now challenged by the vast possibilities for misbehavior that arise in today's networks of electronic communications. People end up seeing pictures, reading words, and indulging in activities that sometimes depart from prevailing community standards. The growing response to these mischievous practices is to implant prohibitions within the electronic hardware and software itself.

Technical Fixes to Social Problems

One example is the V-chip, the device that television manufacturers must now build into every set sold in the United States. The V-chip will enable set owners to block programs with excessive violence or sex. Proponents of the V-chip, including President Bill Clinton, hope it will allow parents to control the kinds of scenes their children see on television.

While giving families power of this kind is a positive development, the V-chip addresses only certain kinds of concerns. For example, many parents I know worry not only about the killing, brutality, and prurient sexuality that abounds on the tube but also the barrage of advertisements that push hollow consumerism as life's central goal. The same technology that spawned the V-chip could also enable a C-chip—a device giving parents the choice of deleting the commercials that bombard kids for 10 minutes out of every half hour. Why is no one promoting such an innovation? (Don't write me. I know the answer.)

Another domain in which the implanting of certain norms is becoming commonplace is the Internet. The Communications Decency Act, before the Supreme Court in 1997 for a ruling on its constitutionality, makes it illegal to send indecent material over the Internet if children may see it.[1] An alternative approach, one that many parents find appealing, involves the use of filtering software. A mini-industry has formed to sell products with names like Net Nanny, Safe Surf, and CyberPatrol. Parents can set these filters to block

1. The Communications Decency Act was declared unconstitutional by the Supreme Court in 1997.

a computer user's access to Web sites that contain pictures of undraped bodies and the like.

Smuggling in Repressive Social Agendas

It turns out, however, that the power of deeply embedded censorship can do more than weed out erotica. In 1997 it was revealed that one of the more popular smut blockers, Cybersitter, also makes it impossible for computers to access the home page of the National Organization for Women. Cybersitter was developed by SolidOak Software in close cooperation with Focus on the Family—a right-wing organization that has waged censorship campaigns seeking to remove books it finds objectionable from libraries and public schools. Thus, Cybersitter is actually an extension of Focus on the Family's antifeminist, antigay, anti-abortion rights agenda.

Smart Filtering?

The next time one of my articles was blocked by filtering software, it was the word "naked," which is used in all kinds of ways, like "the naked truth," "naked ambition." I was writing about a prisoner who was beaten to death in a cowardly and brutal attack by deputy Sheriffs in the L.A. County Jail during a strip search. Although "naked" was blocked, Surf-Watch had no problem with the following sentences: "I'm taking all my clothes off," "I'm not wearing a stitch," and "What's a five-letter word beginning with 'n' and ending with 'd' that means wearing your birthday suit?"

Revolutionary Worker, January 10, 1999.

The utility and seeming neutrality of the package has convinced companies that bundle software to include it in their packages. Do these companies and their customers know the political agenda that they are buying into? SolidOak doesn't conceal its connection to Focus on the Family, but it doesn't advertise it either.

Other filters have also overstepped their advertised purpose. Animal rights and environmental groups complain that CyberPatrol, made by Microsystems Software, blocks their sites because the news and pictures they present are deemed "gross depictions." CyberPatrol also denies access to the League for Programming Freedom (an organization that opposes software patents) and to some 250 newsgroups, including the distinctly nonpornographic offerings of alt.feminism and soc.support.fat-acceptance.

Spying on Loved Ones

In addition to imposing a hidden political agenda, Cybersitter also encourages parents to spy on their children. As SolidOak's press release proclaims, Cybersitter can keep a "secret log" of Internet sites that a user visits, "making it easier for the parent to monitor their children's on-line habits." Other software filters offer similar recordkeeping features.

Products of this kind remind one of the totalitarian states earlier in the nineteenth century that tried to establish order by getting family members to spy on each other. Alas, the same practices could well greet parents when they go off to work. Employers can now deploy programs such as Web Track and Sequel Net Access Manager to monitor their workers' Internet activities and to block access to sites that might detract from productivity.

Both the V-chip and Internet filters reflect today's tendency to respond to legitimate worries with technical fixes. But citizens of cyberspace must learn to identify, criticize and, when necessary, resist the deeply embedded codes in these "protective" devices. Software purchasers should loudly denounce products that try to smuggle in repressive social agendas or limit free speech. Advocacy groups that find themselves blocked by cyberfilters must similarly seize this issue as part of the causes they advance. We must not allow the new technology to become a covert carrier of highly dubious regimes of virtue.

> *"If librarians do not make the case that hardcore pornography should be filtered, then others will make the logical deduction that librarians can't be trusted at all."*

Libraries Should Regulate Internet Access

Mark Y. Herring

Mark Y. Herring contends in the following viewpoint that libraries must install filtering devices on their computers due to the ease with which children can now access pornography on the Internet and become prey to online child molesters. Librarians have always made decisions about what to hold in their libraries, he maintains, and should not be concerned about blocking access to obscene materials. Pornography, he adds, has never been protected by the First Amendment's guarantee of free speech. Mark Y. Herring is dean of library services at Winthrop University in South Carolina.

As you read, consider the following questions:
1. According to Herring, how does the American Library Association define intellectual freedom?
2. How did the *Miller v. California* case modify the *Roth* restrictions regarding obscenity, according to the author?
3. According to the author, what percentage of pornography obtained through libraries is being accessed by underage people?

Reprinted from Mark Y. Herring, "X-Rated Libraries," *The Weekly Standard*, July 5–12, 1999, by permission of *The Weekly Standard*. Copyright, News America Incorporated.

The burning question libraries face today is whether to install filters on the computers they make available to the public for online research. Stumbling now and then onto lascivious material while searching online is practically inevitable and so should be a matter of concern. All sorts of tricks are used to steer innocent users toward pornographic sites. If, for example, you accidentally type "Infoseeck" for "Infoseek" or "Whitehouse.com" for "Whitehouse.gov," you'll get an eyeful of what might be described as presidential activity [such as oral sex]. As regular Internet users are vividly aware, nearly every online search yields at least one pornographic site.

The American Library Association

Yet the American Library Association (ALA), which represents 57,000 librarians, has roundly declined to promote the use of filters to block access to pornographic sites. The ALA isn't even concerned that, by not using filters, libraries make truly enormous amounts of pornography available to young people. Leonard Kniffel, the editor of ALA's official publication for librarians, *American Libraries*, has written, "Kids don't have time to sit at a library computer and troll for smut, nor do they wish to." The constitutional, philosophical, and cultural arguments the ALA has marshalled against filtering are similarly tainted by a weird blend of naivete and ignorance. More important, the ALA's case against filters is just plain wrong.

Filtering, the ALA argues, directly contradicts the First Amendment, ergo, it's wrong, as is *any* form of censorship. This position warps the First Amendment into absolute protection for any and all expression. In its *Intellectual Freedom Manual*, the ALA defines intellectual freedom sweepingly as "the right of any person to believe whatever he wants on any subject, and to express his beliefs or ideas in whatever way he thinks appropriate."

Granted, the Supreme Court has been expansive in its opinions about what speech is, recognizing a range of activities from nude dancing to the wearing of arm bands as protected "speech." This, however, does not amount to First Amendment protection for any and all "speech": Court after court has held that some forms of speech deserve no protection at all.

Some Speech Can Be Censored

Roth v. United States excluded obscenity from the protections accorded to free speech. The plaintiff had developed a lucrative mail order business selling erotic and obscene works, which were quaint in comparison to the online material filtering advocates want to block. Products Roth sold, works like *Photo and Body* and *American Aphrodite Number Thirteen*, were declared unprotected speech. Justice William Brennan, writing for the majority, decided that not only was obscenity "utterly without redeeming social importance," but it falls into the same category as libel and is therefore unprotected.

Reprinted with permission of Chuck Asay and Creators Syndicate.

Roth has been adjusted—most notably by way of the "Roth Test"—but its central argument is still intact. *Miller v. California*, another censorship case, added community standards to *Roth*'s restrictions, placing the burden on communities and local judges. These and other cases have all made the point that the First Amendment is neither absolute nor ambiguous. Since our founding, obscenity and pornography have not been protected forms of speech, regardless of the Court and regardless of the medium used as "speech."

If the First Amendment allows that some forms of speech are not worthy of protection, why then does the ALA condemn filtering? The ALA argues that any restriction on the flow of information is repugnant. To stand for the dissemination of information, the ALA believes, it is necessary to stand against filters. Any limit, then, on the flow of any information is wrong.

Filtering Is a Librarian's Job

This might be a more persuasive principle if librarians didn't violate it every day. I do not know of many libraries that maintain subscriptions to Ku Klux Klan (KKK) materials, or routinely purchase "hate" books from, say, gay-bashing groups. Librarians rightly object to these materials because the "information" contained therein serves no one but the hopelessly unredeemable. Furthermore, librarians often end up restricting information for the most lamentable reason: price. Hardly a librarian alive or dead has not rejected some very valuable resource simply because it cost too much. Budgetary constraints cause libraries to lose good, solid information all the time.

Let's not forget, too, that filtering can be refined to the point where almost no worthwhile information is accidentally filtered. Making such improvements to existing filters may not be easy and may require greater technical expertise. But it *can* be done. Indeed, it is being done and quite successfully. All the same, to argue, as the ALA does, that we must not filter anything for fear of blocking something worthwhile is akin to arguing that we must not prosecute any criminals for fear of convicting the innocent.

Furthermore, it is clear that the ALA has taken a stand against filtering because that appears to be the position of all intelligent people. Everyone knows, after all, that any form of censorship is odious. Yet, the majority of public opinion remains *with* filtering. Even some professional library organizations, such as the Association of College and Research Libraries and the National Commission on Libraries and Information Science have made statements that conflict with ALA's . . . anti-filtering views. It is not too much of a stretch to say that of the 50,000 ALA members, a sizable number are for using filters.

Libraries: Adult Bookstores?

Never in the history of the universe have so many graphic pictures of so much graphic and perverse sexual behavior been available to so many people in so many unprotected situations. Never in the history of the universe has hard-core pornography been available in public libraries. The same images which six months ago only people 21 and older could purchase at "adult bookstores" on the outskirts of town or in the town's red light district, can now be accessed by school children at the public library. Even more disturbing is the fact that this fact goes unmentioned in the local newspaper even after a little girl gets molested at the public library.

E. Michael Jones, *Culture Wars*, July/August 1997.

Librarians have always had to make distinctions between the worthwhile and the worthless. Filtering, you could say, is in their job description. And any librarian who cannot discern an important difference between sexmuseum.com and womenshistory.com clearly does not belong in a library.

Libraries: Chief Purveyors of Pornography

We are fast approaching an epidemic of access to Internet pornography. Cases are now coming to light in which library access to the Internet aided and abetted child-molesters (such as the case of Jack Hornbeck, a convicted child molester who used a Los Angeles public library's Internet connection to distribute child pornography and to arrange sex with children). Moreover, a recent survey by Filtering Facts indicates that 45 percent of all Internet pornography obtained through libraries is being accessed by underage people. Since libraries now offer 50 percent of all Internet access outside the home, they are fast becoming America's chief purveyors of pornography.

If librarians do not make the case that hardcore pornography should be filtered, then others will make the logical deduction that librarians can't be trusted at all. And so, it is especially unfortunate that the ALA, which could have been a voice of reason in this debate, decided to pander to some imagined consensus against filtering. Rather than stand up for the professional prerogatives of its members, the ALA decided to undermine the standing of all librarians, suggesting that they are nothing more than delivery boys ready to pass along every kind of smut available online.

> *"Under this policy [of regulating the Internet], library patrons are all children—even senior citizens. They're all children who want to do something nasty."*

Libraries Should Not Regulate Internet Access

Charles Levendosky

In the following viewpoint, Charles Levendosky maintains that libraries should not regulate Internet access. Using filtering software to protect children from online pornography blocks access to legitimate websites that adult patrons might want to visit, he contends. Levendosky adds that such regulation infringes on patrons' right to freedom of speech and is therefore unconstitutional. Charles Levendosky is the editorial page editor of the *Casper (Wyoming) Star-Tribune* and has a national reputation for First Amendment commentary.

As you read, consider the following questions:
1. To what old high school ritual does Levendosky compare Loudoun County Library's Internet policy?
2. What does Levendosky identify as the main problem with X-Stop filtering software?
3. What are some of the websites that X-Stop has blocked, according to the author?

Reprinted, with permission, from Charles Levendosky, "'Heart of Darkness' Beats to Censor Internet," *Casper (Wyoming) Star-Tribune*, January 8, 1998.

Seldom does one get a peek into the constricted heart of a censor. The new Internet policy for the Loudoun County Public Library in Virginia provides more than a peep—it projects the beat and blood of censorship in shades of inhibited gray.

The library board of trustees, 5-to-4, voted for the new "Policy on Internet Sexual Harassment" in October 1997.

The policy, unless struck down, could become the uptight model for library policies across the nation.

Think of a high school dance in the 1950s when the teachers and chaperones watched couples carefully to see if they were dancing with the proper distance between their young, yearning bodies. Sometimes a teacher would step out on a dance floor and put his arm between a couple. "That distance," he'd intone solemnly. "That distance" is what the library board put between library patrons and the Internet. With that tone. And that solemn judgment.

Treated Like Children

Under this policy, library patrons are all children—even senior citizens. They're all children who want to do something nasty. The trustees approved a policy that prohibits e-mail, chat rooms, news groups, and sexual content that might be deemed harmful to juveniles. That is, the policy forbids—to adults—information that is legal for adults under the First Amendment

Too bad, said John Nicholas, chairman of the board of trustees. The library doesn't have to provide everything, he added.

When Congress passed the Communications Decency Act in 1996 in an attempt to reduce communications on the Internet to the level of a child, the U.S. Supreme Court in 1997 said Congress had violated the First Amendment. The high court's ruling gave the speaker on the Internet all the protections that any publisher or street corner pamphleteer has—the highest First Amendment protection. But now the Loudoun County Public Library Board of Trustees is attempting to reduce the information that one receives through the Internet to the level of a child.

Never mind that the Supreme Court was protecting a major new form of publishing and distributing. Obviously, the library board doesn't believe their adult patrons have the right to receive adult communications this way.

Preventing Sexual Harassment?

The policy talks about protecting patrons and staff from sexual harassment that might occur if sexual content appears on a computer terminal. Yet the new policy demands that their Internet computers must "be installed in close proximity to, and in full view of, library staff." No privacy screens on the terminals are permitted. Whatever you have on the screen, anyone can read over your shoulder.

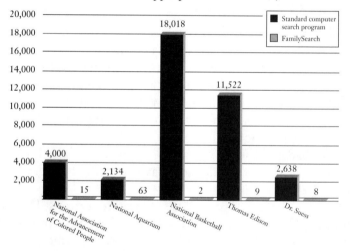

Computerized Censor Casts Too Wide a Net

Difference in number of documents accessed on the Internet for various search terms, using standard computer search programs and using FamilySearch, a search program intended to block access to material deemed inappropriate for children, 1997

Source: *Faulty Filters: How Content Filters Block Access to Kid-Friendly Information on the Internet.* Electronic Privacy Information Center, December 1997 (www.epic.org/reports/filter-report.html).

Imagine now a former day, when you might have gone to the library to read something about venereal disease in a library reference book—and suddenly a loudspeaker broadcasts every word you are reading to the entire room. Would you want to read at the public library? It would shut down curiosity. It slams the door on information that might be very important personally.

No privacy. Who knows what the library patrons might be seeking in this bright day of a new communications medium.

Too bad, according to Nicholas. Some nearby libraries that have their Internet terminals in private rooms, he claimed, have been used to bring up sexual content. He didn't specify whether that meant information about condoms or the mating habits of the green-toed gecko.

Learning Brings Disobedience and Heresy

Sounds a lot like Virginia before the American Revolution, when Royal Governor William Berkeley wrote in the 1640s: "I thank God there are no free schools nor printing; and I hope we shall not have these for hundreds of years; for learning has brought disobedience and heresy. . . ."

But the Internet is here. And in the Loudoun County Public Library if you search out some information that has a sexual tinge, be careful or you might be charged with creating a sexually hostile environment.

The library board purchased a Web site blocking software program called X-Stop to filter and block out unwanted pornography sites from their Internet terminals. Trouble is, the board doesn't know what X-Stop blocks. Nicholas doesn't know. Neither does Michael Bradshaw, the CEO of Log-On Data Corporation which makes X-Stop. By error, he said, X-Stop blocks more than 350 sites that it wasn't intended to block.

Naughty! Naughty!

A number of library patrons who feel their access to information has been denied by this policy filed a lawsuit against the library board of trustees. The lawsuit names a number of significant Web sites that have been blocked by X-Stop: Society of Friends (Quakers) Home page, Yale University biology graduate school, Zero Population Growth, Safer Sex Education, National Journal on Sexual Orientation Law, AIDS quilt, Heritage Foundation, American Association of University Women-Maryland branch, and others.

Nicholas says that the library has the right to select the material it offers the public and X-Stop does that. But that isn't selection, that's de-selection.

Filtering Bias

The library filtering software X-Stop . . . blocked access to a wide range of information on breast cancer, sex education, gay and lesbian rights, as well as web sites sponsored by organizations like the Quakers and the Biology Department at Yale University. At the same time, X-Stop did not censor all sites that discussed sex, indicating a product flaw or manufacturer's bias. For example, X-Stop did not block web sites that publish material opposing homosexuality, favoring Internet censorship, or promoting abstinence rather than safe sex practices.

Michael deCourcy Hinds, *Protecting Our Rights: What Goes on the Internet*, 1998.

Many librarians, as professionals, take pride in their selection of books and materials so that it is inclusive and balanced. This process—turned over to a private company that uses an automated software program to exclude material—cannot be called a selection process without mangling the English language.

No one knows what, in the universe of cyberspace, has been de-selected or why. Not Nicholas, not Bradshaw.

A library patron who wants to use the Internet computers must surrender his or her library card and sign a copy of the policy. May I have your passport, please?

If a patron attempts to call up a blocked site, the screen flashes:

"Violation!! Violation!! Violation!!"

Naughty, naughty. Librarian will spank your hands.

If the patron continues to call up blocked Web sites—and how would you know since no one does?—he or she will be told to leave the library. If the patron refuses, the police will be called. And the patron will be charged with trespass.

This is Loudoun County's friendly neighborhood library—home of the censor and the censor's dark heart.

Editor's note: In November 1998, the library board was found guilty of violating the First Amendment and, as a result, the policy was dropped.

Periodical Bibliography

The following articles have been selected to supplement the diverse views presented in this chapter. Addresses are provided for periodicals not indexed in the *Readers' Guide to Periodical Literature*, the *Alternative Press Index*, the *Social Sciences Index*, or the *Index to Legal Periodicals and Books*.

Jonathan Curiel	"Cyberporn vs. Censorship," *Advocate*, May 13, 1997.
Amitai Etzioni	"ACLU Favors Porn Over Parents," *Wall Street Journal*, October 14, 1998.
Lisa Guernsey	"Sticks and Stones Can Hurt, but Bad Words Pay," *The New York Times*, April 8, 1999.
Marjorie Heins	"Screening Out Sex: Kids, Computers, and the New Censors," *American Prospect*, July/August 1998.
J.D. Lasica	"Censorship Devices on the Internet," *American Journalism Review*, September 1997.
Joshua Micah Marshall	"Will Free Speech Get Tangled in the Net?" *American Prospect*, January/February 1998.
Michael Meyer	"A Bad Dream Comes True in Cyberspace," *Newsweek*, January 8, 1996.
Neil Munro	"Quiet in the Library! Children Viewing Porn," *Weekly Standard*, December 22, 1997. Available from 1211 Avenue of the Americas, New York, NY 10036.
National Review	"Internet: The Lost Fight," August 11, 1997.
Carl Rowan	"Protecting Kids from the Internet," *Liberal Opinion Week*, January 25, 1999. Available from 108 E. Fifth St., Vinton, IA 52349.
Jube Shiver Jr., David G. Savage, and Elizabeth Shogren	"Law Curbing Indecency on Internet Overturned," *Los Angeles Times*, June 27, 1997. Available from Times Mirror Square, Los Angeles, CA 90053.

CHAPTER 4

What Should Be the Feminist Stance on Pornography?

Chapter Preface

The protracted study of pornography's effect on women has led to a heated debate within the women's movement between those who oppose pornography and those who defend it. According to writer Edward H. Hurley, the history of the feminist response to pornography can be divided up into three "waves."

During the first wave of the feminist critique of pornography, which began in the early 1970s, feminists such as Gloria Steinem viewed pornography as a means of objectifying women and sex. Others, such as Helen Longini, stressed that pornography degraded women. First wave feminists claimed that pornography—as opposed to erotica—portrayed women in a demeaning way.

In the 1970s, however, this mainstream feminist stance gave way to the more radical view that pornography subordinated women and therefore enforced gender inequality. Radical anti-pornography feminists argued that porn not only caused sexual violence against women, it *was* sexual violence. Writer Andrea Dworkin and attorney Catharine MacKinnon have articulated this view most forcefully. MacKinnon writes, "from the testimony of the pornography, what men want is: women bound, women battered, women tortured, women humiliated, women degraded and defiled."

Finally, many third-wave feminists defend pornography. Feminists such as Nadine Strossen, president of the American Civil Liberties Union, argue that suppressing *any* speech inevitably leads to political repression. Strossen claims that "censorship is a dangerous weapon which, if permitted, would inevitably be turned against [women]." Some feminists believe that pornography harms women but argue that censoring it would lead to the suppression of other sexual information regarding birth control and abortion. In addition, many third-wave feminists argue that pornography promotes sexual freedom for women and is therefore beneficial.

The feminist response to pornography has been complicated by opposing views within the women's movement. The authors in the following chapter debate what the feminist stance should be on pornography.

> "In confronting the sexual domination of women in pornography [feminists] had unwittingly hit the jugular vein—or perhaps, more accurately, the nerve centre—of male supremacy."

Feminists Should Oppose Pornography

John Stoltenberg

John Stoltenberg is the cofounder of the feminist organization Men Against Pornography. In the following viewpoint, Stoltenberg urges feminists to continue their history of fighting pornography because of its harmful effects on women. He claims that pornography has become more violent and sadistic over the years, and has become increasingly accessible. Stoltenberg maintains that fighting pornography is crucial to fighting male supremacy, which denies women freedom and justice.

As you read, consider the following questions:
1. What event does Stoltenberg claim is the origin of anti-pornography feminist activism?
2. What effect does pornography have on men, according to the controlled experiments that the author cites?
3. What does Linda Marchiano claim happened to her while working in the pornography industry?

Excerpted from John Stoltenberg, *Refusing to Be a Man: Essays on Sex and Justice*, rev. ed. (London: UCL Press, 2000). Reprinted by permission of the Taylor & Francis Group.

The idea of confronting pornography as a civil-rights issue did not fall from the sky. It grew out of the outrage and frustration of over a decade of grassroots feminist activism against pornography. The definitive history of this influential movement has yet to be written—but here's a sketch:

Playboy and Miss America

Activism in the women's movement on the issue of pornography can be traced back to September 1968, when women, led by a group called New York Radical Women, first 'zapped' the Miss America Pageant in Atlantic City, with days of songs, chants, and guerilla theatre protesting the contest's sexist and racist celebration of women as objects.

A rash of demonstrations against Hugh M. Hefner's *Playboy* empire soon followed at Playboy Clubs across the country. One group of protesters, the Mountain Moving Day Brigade, challenged Hefner's hegemony in these words:

> We sisters join together to fight you, your *Playboy* empire and everything you represent, and we shall build instead a society in which women and men are free to relate to each other as human beings of dignity and worth. Until you no longer oppose this, you shall have no peace.

Hefner, for his part, issued an in-house memo that got leaked to the nation:

> These chicks are our natural enemy. . . . It is time we do battle with them. . . . What I want is a devastating piece that takes the militant feminists apart. They are unalterably opposed to the romantic boy-girl society that *Playboy* promotes. . . . Let's go to it and make it a real winner.

It was all-out war: the pornographers against women, women against the pornographers. In the next several years, there were to be scores of scattered feminist anti-pornography actions, including, for the first time, civil disobedience: In the spring of 1970, militant feminists seized and barricaded the executive offices of the avant-garde, Left/liberal Grove Press in New York City, partly as a protest against its publications that degraded women. . . .

The year 1976 marks a sort of flash point in the feminist anti-pornography movement. In February, a first-run theatre in New York City's Times Square opened a movie called *Snuff*, which purported to show the actual murder of a woman for sexual entertainment. Hundreds of women and some men picketed the theatre night after night. In the movie, a man kills then disembowels a woman and holds up her uterus as he appears to have an orgasm. Eventually, the gore was revealed to be simulated but hoax or not, the movie sent out a message about women that was all too real. When *Snuff* rolled out into national distribution, it galvanized feminists to form local groups against pornography across the United States—the largest of which, Women Against Violence in Pornography and Media (WAVPM), was based in San Francisco.

In June 1976, Atlantic Records erected a billboard in Los Angeles on Sunset Strip showing a woman bound and bruised saying "I'm 'Black and Blue' from the Rolling Stones—and I love it!" A group called Women Against Violence Against Women (WAVAW) protested and got the billboard taken down, then joined with California National Organization for Women (NOW) in calling a national boycott against Atlantic, Warner Bros. and Elektra/Asylum records, demanding an end to these companies' violent and woman-hating album covers.

When the June 1978 issue of Larry Flynt's *Hustler* magazine hit newsstands, it triggered another outburst of feminist protests coast-to-coast. Billing itself an 'all-meat issue', the cover showed a naked woman being shoved head-first into a meat grinder—and extruded at the other end as raw hamburger.

The first feminist conference on pornography convened in San Francisco in November 1978, sponsored by WAVPM, and it launched the first Take Back the Night March—down San Francisco's pornography row in North Beach. A few months later, in October 1979, over 5,000 women and men marched against pornography in Times Square, organized by Women Against Pornography, originally a WAVPM spinoff. In the years thereafter, Take Back the Night marches and rallies have become an annual event in hundreds of cities and communities. Dozens of WAVAW chapters and many other groups sprang up in local protests against record-album jackets, pornography retailers, and other forms of media exploitation and violence against women. In addition, on hundreds of campuses, there were spontaneous demonstrations against fraternity and film-society showings of pornographic films, the sale of pornographic magazines in campus bookstores, and photographers soliciting for women to pose for *Playboy*.

Woman-Hating Propaganda

This burgeoning grass-roots activism was accompanied by a surge of feminist writings that analyzed pornography as sexist, degrading, demeaning images and as woman-hating propaganda. As feminists spoke out, more and more women came forward and told how men's use of pornography had been directly involved in their personal histories of incest, child sexual abuse, marital rape, battery, and other forms of sexual victimization, or how pornography had been used to season them into a life of prostitution.

Men Are Still on Top

Most pornography contains a cruel message, sometimes overt, sometimes hidden. The suggestion is that women should not only be sexually conquered, but beaten, tortured, and enslaved—triumphed over in any way.

Pornography is loaded with attacks on feminism. Men are told to reassert their mastery over women. Perhaps this explains why porn is booming. Even if the consumer grows bored with the explicit material, he may still continue buying for the ego-soothing message that men are still on top.

Michael Betzold, *For Men Against Sexism: A Book of Readings.* Ed. Jon Snodgrass. Albion, CA: Times Change Press, 1977.

By the beginning of the 1980s, a new political analysis was emerging: a real-life based comprehension of pornography as being somehow central to women's inferior social status—together with a sense of being utterly powerless against the resources of the huge pornography industry and its callous civil-libertarian defenders. . . .

More Brutality

In addition to this background of feminist anti-pornography activism, the thinking behind the civil-rights anti-pornography law was influenced by:
* The increased distribution of pornography, due in part

to technologic advances such as cable TV and the home video market.

- The wider availability of more and more violent and sadistic pornography. Acts were being photographed and sold that were heretofore unimaginable: torture, mutilation, sex with animals, vaginal penetration by knives, and so forth. Pornography production seemed to be racing to keep ahead of the satiation effect in consumers—trying to deliver a sex kick to sated would-be satyrs through more and more brutality against women.

- Social-science research designed to test hypotheses suggested by feminists analysis of pornography. Controlled experiments were conducted with groups of 'normal' college-age men, screened to eliminate 'rape-prone' and 'high-hostile' types. The experiments showed that in these average good joes, exposure to certain types of pornography produced significant effects such as increased levels of aggression and hostility, increased callousness toward women, and increased self-reported likelihood to rape if they thought they would not get caught.

- The escape of 'Linda Lovelace', whose real name is Linda Marchiano. In her autobiography, the woman who starred in *Deep Throat*, the world's highest-grossing pornographic film, told how she had in fact been intimidated, beaten, and brutally bullied into performing for pornography by her pimp/husband—sometimes at gunpoint. For several years Marchiano tried to get someone to help her take her case to court, but no one in the succession of male lawyers she appealed to thought anything could be done.

- Then, beginning in June 1980, when Linda Marchiano joined with Women Against Pornography in calling for a nationwide boycott of *Deep Throat*, Andrea Dworkin, the radical feminist writer, and Catharine A. MacKinnon, at the time a feminist lawyer teaching at Yale Law School, attempted to help Marchiano take legal action against the gross injustice she had experienced. The statutes of limitation in the crimes of abuse that had happened to her had by now expired—as indeed they usually do before a woman so sexually victimized can recover enough emotionally to be able to cope with a prosecution. Meanwhile the film of her coerced performance continues to earn its owners and distributors millions and millions of dollars.

- The backlash reaction against feminist anti-pornography activists from pornographers and defenders of pornography: Feminists who had organized and written against pornography during the 70s had no idea just HOW central pornography was to the system of men's social power over and against women. But the misogyny and vehemence with which their movement began to be denounced and reviled, in pornography magazines and elsewhere, became a tangible tip-off that in confronting the sexual domination of women in pornography they had unwittingly hit the jugular vein—or perhaps, more accurately, the nerve centre—of male supremacy. . . .

Freedom and Equality

Historically, when people have not had justice and when people have not had freedom, they have had only the material reality of injustice and unfreedom. When freedom and justice don't exist, they're but a dream and a vision, an abstract idea longed for. You can't really know what justice would be like or what freedom would feel like. You can only know how it feels NOT to have them, and what it feels like to hope, to imagine, to desire them with a passion. Sexual freedom is an idea whose time has NOT come. It can't possibly be truly experienced until there is sexual justice. And sexual justice is incompatible with a definition of freedom that is based on the subordination of women.

Equality is still a 'radical' idea. It makes some people very angry. It also gives some people hope.

When equality is an idea whose time HAS come, we will perhaps know sex with justice, we will perhaps know passion with compassion, we will perhaps know ardor and affection with honor. In that time, when the integrity within everyone's body and the whole personhood of each person is celebrated whenever two people touch, we will perhaps truly know the freedom to be sexual in a world of real equality.

According to pornography, you can't get there from here. According to male supremacy, you should not even want to try.

Some of us want to go there. Some of us want to be there. And we know that the struggle will be difficult and long. But we know that the passion for justice cannot be denied. And someday—SOMEDAY—there will be both justice and freedom for each person—and thereby for us all.

"Feminists opposed to anti-pornography legislation argue that it threatens to close down spaces which women are still trying to open up in exploring how to represent themselves as sexual agents."

Feminists Should Not Oppose Pornography

Lynne Segal

Lynne Segal is professor of psychology and gender studies at Birkbeck College, University of London. Segal argues in the following viewpoint that feminists should not oppose pornography because such efforts divert attention away from the real cause of women's subordination: institutional patriarchy. She claims that contrary to the claims of anti-pornography feminists, most pornography does not depict violence or cause sex crimes against women. Feminists should focus their efforts on changing the basic cultural institutions that cause misogyny and oppression, Segal contends.

As you read, consider the following questions:

1. What flaws in the anti-pornography argument does Segal criticize?
2. According to Judith Butler, what is the function of pornography?
3. What effect did the Butler decision have on pornography sold in Canada?

Excerpted from Lynne Segal, "Pornographic Battles." This article originally appeared in volume 2, 2000, of *Index on Censorship*, the international magazine of free expression. For more information, visit www.indexoncensorship.org. Reprinted with permission.

Within feminism, battles over pornography have become the wars without end. We thought it had peaked in the USA in the 1980s, but the cannons are still firing. Despite the controversy their campaigns generate, those who see pornography as pivotal to women's oppression have built a popular base for anti-pornography feminism, and continue to make inroads into legal frameworks. This is why the issue of 'pornography' will not go away. From the close of the 1970s, it became impossible to write about sexuality, as a feminist, without being hijacked by, and forced to take a stand on, the issue of pornography. . . .

Male Sexuality and Domination

In the women's liberation movement of the 1970s the analysis and politics of sexuality were always accorded a central place. Feminists initially sought to celebrate female sexuality: liberating it from male-centred discourses and sexist practices to uncover women's own 'autonomous' sexuality. However, early ideas linking women's liberation to greater sexual confidence were soon overshadowed by the pressure of challenging the seeming tenacity of men's power over women. From the close of the 1970s, forceful feminist writing was insisting that predatory male sexuality was the overriding source of that power, and naming pornography as its chief incitement. Male 'sexuality' was irrevocably fused to 'domination', redefined as an urge to power.

Other feminists, as I did, saw these moves as part of a reaction to more conservative times and the setbacks faced by feminist activism—especially in the USA, where anti-pornography feminism arose at the close of the 1970s. Isolating sexuality and men's violence from other issues of women's inequality was not only a defensive tactic for women, but one closest to the rising tide of conservative backlash against radical politics generally. The Right has always liked to demonise sexuality, seeing it as the source of all our ills. Some feminists were now joining them.

The new feminist discourses against pornography were strengthened in 1987 when Catharine MacKinnon published *Feminism Unmodified: Discourses on Life and Law*. This added legal arguments to Andrea Dworkin's earlier indictment of pornography in *Pornography: Men Possessing Women*, published in 1981, which depicted pornography as men's literal domination and torture of women. MacKinnon declared pornography a 'violation of women's civil rights', arguing that it convinces men that women are inferior. Pornography should be seen as not merely a form of representation—sexist and offensive images or words—but as *literally* harming women and creating gender inequality. It causes men to injure and violate women both in its creation (a claim passionately and repeatedly rebutted by many sex workers themselves) and in its consumption: teaching men to injure and debase women through linking their sexual arousal to degrading images of women.

A Convenient Scapegoat

The women's liberation movement was not concerned primarily with censorship, either for or against. Rather, feminists saw cultural production of all kinds as a site for feminist struggle to authorise and encourage silenced voices. That said, feminist anti-pornography arguments are seductive because most mainstream pornography purveys blatantly sexist (and often racist) imagery. Pornography's standard servicing of men's narcissistic fantasies of female sexual availability is a continuing provocation when sexual harassment and rape remain endemic. It seems to offer a convenient scapegoat for rage against such abuses. Convenient, but hazardous.

It is hazardous because the argument that it is commercial pornography that underlies the subordination and abuse of women in society is seriously misleading. First of all, anti-pornography feminism has systematically misrepresented the content of mainstream pornography as 'violence'. Secondly, it has consistently misrepresented studies of effects of pornography, falsely claiming they offer consistent and conclusive proof that pornographic images cause sex crimes. Thirdly, it disavows our knowledge of the peculiar nature of fantasy, with its complex, often contradictory, relation to actual behaviour. Fourthly, it eschews recent theories of representation, which reveal that meaning is seen as never simply fixed in advance, but determined by its broader discursive context as well as its specific interpretive audience. Finally, and most fundamentally of all, anti-pornography feminism fails to address the elementary point that the role of commercial pornography in depicting a crude, imperious and promiscuous male sexuality, alongside female receptivity and vulnerability, is *completely* overshadowed by, and *entirely* dependent on, the official discourses and imagery of science, medicine, religion and mainstream cultural productions (high or low), prevalent all around us.

Gender Hierarchy and Oppression

While many may find the sexually explicit messages of commercial pornography offensive, in fact they mimic—yet also sometimes unsettle—the ways in which the most authoritative, revered, even sacred discourses of our culture depict women as subordinate, sexually passive and sexually available. There have, for example, been feminist critiques of the 'great' paintings of western art along these lines, and illustrations could be drawn from a whole range of genres. Many fields of knowledge rely on a taken-for-granted view of unalterable gender difference that does, in the end, imply the subordination of women. This is nowhere more prominent than in the recent flowering of 'new evolutionary theory', which flaunts its account of men's ever-ready sexual desire.

Match the advertisement with the product it advertises:

- a. Beer
- b. Jeans
- c. Perfume
- d. Diet clinics
- e. Plastic surgery
- f. Breast implants

KIRK →92

Reprinted by permission of Kirk Anderson.

Yet as sex therapists are all too well aware, the sexist meta-phors and phallic hubris, both of recent scientific discourse and of traditional pornography, are far from reflecting a real world in which the male member is permanently erect and endlessly ready for unencumbered sex.

In her recent analysis of pornography, *Excitable Speech: A Politics of the Performative*, Judith Butler explores this failure of expectations. She suggests that pornography depicts just those 'unrealizable positions' that predetermine our social expectations of gender behaviour. Pornography in no way constructs that social reality; on the contrary, it serves to mock the impossible distance between gender norms and actual practices.

Nobody needs pornography to remind them of the hierar-chical 'truths' of sexual difference. Some, indeed, turn to it to escape them, identifying with who-knows-what position of domination or subjection as they gaze upon its products. It is dominant ideology itself, with its obsessive disdain for what it regards as the gross material body and its functions—of se-cretions, odours and open orifices; perspiration, pulpy flesh and fluctuating organs—which works to produce the quite inevitable pull of the tauntingly illicit.

No Correlation Between Porn and Sex Crimes

Pornography is thus only one of many phallocentric and misogynistic discourses that fashion our images of gender and sexuality—and the least esteemed, least convincing, often most contradictory one. Those who most eagerly insist on its unique offensiveness face the problem that surveys of what is packaged as pornography show that violent imagery is rare, rather than definitive of the genre, as anti-porn feminists claim. Moreover, men are more likely than women to be de-picted as 'submissive' in the S&M or bondage imagery avail-able. This means, of course, that were there any truth in our direct mimicry of the pornographic, feminists might well feel that they should be out fly-posting this well-established dominatrix pornography, rather than trying to eliminate it. A host of empirical inquiries, from the Netherlands, Swe-den, Denmark or the USA, have all failed to find any con-sistent correlation between the availability of pornography

Pornography: A Symptom, Not a Cause

I think I understand where the rage of anti-porn activists comes from. I, too, feel the weight of sexism. I, too, struggle against its definitions. I share a vulnerability to violence at the hands of men. And I know how tempting it is to wallow in helplessness before representations of that rage. But trying to destroy dangerous art is like shooting at a rainbow, you can never hit the source. No sooner do you succeed at banning one offensive work than others, more covert, arise. The intention remains intact and all the more dangerous for the illusion that, in attaining power over a text, we have managed to control the condition it describes.

Richard Goldstein, *Village Voice*, 1984.

and sex crimes against women, many indeed have found negative correlations (not that this tells us anything about causality either). Overall, the main finding from the avalanche of correlational studies carried out over the last 20 years is that they are inconsistent, both with each other and with the claims of anti-pornography texts.

The Butler Decision

Nevertheless, it was anti-pornography campaigners, rather than their critics, who had most success in shifting the legal debate in favour of censorship during the 1990s. They boosted their appeal by joining forces with others campaigning against the less contentious injuries of 'Hate Speech' now flourishing in the USA, a move documented by Mari Matsuda and others in the 1993 *Words that Wound*. It is over a decade since MacKinnon and Dworkin first drafted their Model Ordinance, arguing that women can assert their civil rights and become fully human *only* once they win the battle against pornography. The Ordinance classifies pornography as sex discrimination ('the graphic sexually explicit subordination of women through pictures or words') and urges those who have suffered 'harm' from it to seek damages through the courts from its makers, sellers and distributors—public or private. After initial success in Minneapolis, the Ordinance was eventually defeated in various states of the USA following prolonged legal battles, but in Canada anti-pornography feminists (assisted by MacKinnon) were victorious, with the adoption of a modified version of the Ordinance in the Butler Supreme Court decision in 1992.

Other feminists, who have—often reluctantly—felt compelled to fight the Ordinance, in and outside the courts, argue that the relentless pursuit of such legislative change is dangerous. It relies upon vague and ambiguous terms which are certain to backfire against the sexually powerless it supposedly protects. Their fears have been realised, at least according to those who have been monitoring the effects of the Canadian legislation. Since the Butler decision, straight mainstream pornography is flourishing. Representations of alternative sexualities, by contrast, are facing increasingly intense censorship according to a study made by Brenda Cossman *et al, Bad Attitudes on Trial: Pornography Feminism and the Butler Decision*. The misappropriation of this new Canadian law, not against many men's cosily familiar sexist pornography, but rather against the more unsettling productions of sexual minorites which might work to subvert them, has been the precise and predictable outcome.

In the area of race, similar predictable reversals have occurred. The speech of the powerful remains protected (as before), the speech of minorities gets censored. Thus it is the performances of black rap groups, 2 Live Crew and Salt 'n' Pepa which have recently been targeted for censorship in US courts. As others have noticed, this strengthens the racism of conservative critics, such as Stephen Macedo, who has declared that 'rap' is the special contribution of blacks to 'American cultural degeneration'. New obscenity legislation can be a dangerous thing in its strengthening of legal powers to discriminate against the productions of unpopular cultural minorities. This is why feminists opposed to anti-pornography legislation argue that it threatens to close down spaces which women are still trying to open up in exploring how to represent themselves as sexual agents. From this perspective, the last thing we want to do is to fix the meanings of words and images independently from seeking to understand their social context and audiences.

"The greatest damage done by the cult of conservative [anti-pornography] feminism may be the way it has sought to hijack feminism itself."

Anti-Pornography Feminists Harm the Women's Movement

Carol Queen

Carol Queen is the author of *Real Live Nude Girl: Chronicles of Sex-Positive Culture*. In the following viewpoint, Queen argues that conservative anti-porn feminists have harmed the women's movement. She contends that anti-porn feminists have portrayed women as powerless victims and have worked against sexual freedom for women. Most important, Queen asserts that anti-pornography feminism has silenced the voices of other feminists who disagree that pornography degrades women and causes sexual violence against them.

As you read, consider the following questions:
1. How do anti-pornography feminists view sex, according to Queen?
2. What did the "-apolis ordinances" seek to do, according to the author?
3. According to Queen, what was the aftermath of Canada's Butler decision?

Reprinted from Carol Queen, "The Cult of Conservative Feminism," *Gauntlet*, vol. 2, 1997, by permission of the author.

Feminism has been schizophrenic about sexuality at least since the days of Victoria Woodhull and Tennessee Claflin a century ago, who—unlike representatives of mainstream organizations, who saw unbridled sexuality as dangerous to women—associated women's betterment with free love. Contemporary feminism is just as split, with disproportionate media attention going to feminists who are suspicious of, if not downright hostile to, sexual expression and many types of sexual diversity. These feminists are associated, in particular, with the anti-pornography and anti-sex work points of view. They tend also to have the most negative possible read on sadomasochism (S/M). By contrast, many feminists identify as "pro-sex" or "sex-positive," decrying censorship, supporting sex workers, and generally seeming the opposite of their putative sisters who are less libertarian or liberationist in their views of sex.

Pro-Sex and Anti-Sex Feminists

Some pro-sex feminists' politics devolve from their pro-choice sentiments; they agree, for example, when prostitutes argue that their right to control their own bodies extends as certainly to sexual choices as to reproductive ones. As porn star Nina Hartley has pointed out, her youthful understanding of feminism left her with the impression that a woman should be able to do with her body as she pleased—including finding sexual satisfaction wherever she desired it, and extending to using her body to make porn. Others are fundamentally anti-censorship, feeling that censorship never serves women and is often aimed at silencing feminist voices.

Other feminists see sexual behavior first and foremost as a locus, potential or actual, of gender oppression. From this perspective, sex is a problem, not a pleasure. The oppression-oriented viewpoint is concerned with reproductive health and freedom, rape and abuse, sexual harassment, and other issues in which sex is, or can be, a problem. In this view, pornography is not an erotic documentation of sexual behavior and fantasy, it is material meant to indoctrinate women into sexual practices that men, not women, enjoy and to convince men that women are best treated as sexual objects. Prostitution is never choice-based and is always degrading.

Feminism at Odds with Itself

These opposing views have a real impact on some women's willingness to identify as feminist. Many have shied away from the label largely based on their reaction to conservative feminism, which, they may feel, denigrates or does not support their desires, behavior, or their sense of their own femininity. This situation is exacerbated by the position of the media, which tends to play up conservative feminist perspectives, especially the power team of Andrea Dworkin and Catharine MacKinnon. This pandering is not progressive, as we will see below. It results in a populace which does not know there is a strong feminist movement that opposes the Dworkin/MacKinnon view, cutting women off from pro-sex feminism.

Anyone, feminist or not, who believes feminism has a monolithic and uncomplicated picture of sexuality, is incorrect. This could not, in fact, be further from the truth. Feminist thought and politics mirrors the antipathy many women feel about sex. On the one hand, many feminists have been outspokenly pro-sex education and pro-sexual choice. Many activists for sexual liberation have been outspokenly pro-feminist. Feminist classics like *Our Bodies, Ourselves* and Betty Dodson's *Liberating Masturbation* (now reissued as *Sex For One)* arm women with information about their bodies and about their sexual choices. Pro-sex organizations with their roots in feminism arose, like the sex worker's rights group COYOTE (Call Off Your Old Tired Ethics), the Feminist Anti-Censorship Task Force (FACT), and Feminists for Free Expression. These groups have sometimes worked in coalition with more mainstream women's organizations; COYOTE, for example, twice convinced the National Organization for Women to pass resolutions calling for the decriminalization of prostitution.

Discomfort and Hostility

But sexuality has also made mainstream feminists profoundly uncomfortable. Lesbians, the "lavender menace," were initially made to feel unwelcome by heterosexual feminists. When Betty Dodson showed slides of vulvas to a group of women at a national National Organization for

Women (NOW) conference in the early 1970s, many women walked out. Judy Chicago's beautiful and audacious art installation *The Dinner Party*, featuring a table set with plates decorated with vulvar imagery, got mixed reviews from feminists in that decade, even as women were decorating their apartments with prints of Georgia O'Keefe's subtler labial flowers. When Good Vibrations, a women-owned sex store, attempted to place an ad in *Ms.* magazine a decade later they were refused because, *Ms.*'s representative explained, "We're not a sex magazine." (Ironically, *Playboy* magazine refused Good Vibrations advertising at about the same time.)

Other examples display not just discomfort, but sometimes overt hostility. Women Against Violence and Pornography in Media (WAVPM), which organized to draw attention to misogynist images, soon dropped its mainstream media focus and transmogrified into Women Against Pornography (WAP). FACT came into being to counter WAP's one-sided picture of explicit media. In the early 1980s Barnard College co-sponsored a conference about women and sexuality which became a bitter battleground for the two factions, with conservative feminists pressuring Barnard to cancel the conference and outing some presenters' S/M interests. Take Back the Night marches became another locus of disagreement, pitting feminists who associated violence with porn and the sex industry against sex workers who were furious that they and their workplaces were being targeted.

Conservative feminism inherited the mantle of the 1950s mother who warned that "men only want one thing" and the Victorian certitude that women need to be protected. It also became the group that could most vociferously express American antipathy about sex, explicit media, and sexual freedom, all under the increasingly socially acceptable rubric of feminism. When today's feminists express concern about a backlash against feminism, they often fail to see that this backlash is powered in part by people's response to the visibility of conservative, anti-sex feminism, which has tended to put the blame for sexual problems on men and which has failed to support women in their desires for sexual independence and exploration. But conservative feminism (and by extension, I believe, the backlash against it) has also been powered by personalities: in particular, by four women who have associated themselves inextricably with the feminist fight against pornography and sex work—Andrea Dworkin, Catharine MacKinnon, Diana Russell, and Kathleen Barry.

Andrea Dworkin

Dworkin came to prominence within feminism in the 1970s with her book *Woman Hating,* which sought to document systemic misogyny. A brilliant rhetorician, she was already naming pornography a source of oppression of women. This perspective was developed further in *Pornography: Men Possessing Women.* Perhaps most interesting from a Dworkin-watcher's point of view is her book *Right Wing Women,* a rather sympathetic analysis of the social and political concerns of female right-wing activists. Given the way some of these women would subsequently form coalitions with conservative feminists, this work—which was greeted with some surprise in feminist circles when it was first published—seems, in retrospect, completely strategic.

Dworkin upped the ante considerably with her book *Intercourse,* published in 1986, which posits that in a patriarchal society there can be no penetration of women which is not rape. Feminism is still trying to live down the ridicule and bad press generated in its name by *Intercourse.* The book received more mainstream attention than any of Dworkin's previous works.

The Dworkin-MacKinnon Team

However, Dworkin teamed up with a partner who would help her reinvent herself in the public eye—Catharine MacKinnon. An attorney and the daughter of a powerful conservative Midwestern judge, MacKinnon, with Dworkin, began attempting to dismantle pornography through legislative means, authoring and shepherding through "the -apolis ordinances" in first Minneapolis, MN, and then Indianapolis, IN, in 1983. These ordinances, subsequently overturned as unconstitutional, sought to redefine pornography as matter which depicts the degradation of women and children (even though most porn depicts no such thing) and which is therefore harmful and actionable. The -apolis laws would have allowed a woman who claimed to have been harmed by pornography—either in its making, or by a man who was ostensibly motivated by porn to rape or abuse her—to recover damages in civil court from the maker *and* distributor of the porn.

Civil libertarians, First Amendment advocates, and pro-sex feminists spoke out immediately against the vague wording of these laws, as well as their attempt to bring criminal matters into civil court and to spread the blame for criminal behavior to people such as video store clerks who had nothing whatsoever to do with it. Critics also feared that this attempt to spread responsibility to other parties might be used as a defense by the actual culprits, as rapists learned they were being given a feminist seal of approval for blaming someone or something else for their crimes.

Even after municipal defeats, these ordinances were raised from the dead in the guise of the federal Pornography Victims' Compensation Act,[1] and there is some indication that similar politicking has taken place at the United Nations.

The Butler Decision

Dworkin and MacKinnon's most successful instance of international politicking to date is Canada's 1992 Butler Decision. With Butler, Canada overturned its standing body of obscenity-related law (which was similar to that of the United States and emphasized community standards) and redefined obscenity as material which depicts violent treatment or degradation of women and children. The language, put forward by a MacKinnon/Dworkin-influenced Canadian women's group called LEAF, closely resembles the definitions written into the "-apolis ordinances."

Among many other anti-censorship feminist reasons to oppose this definition of obscenity, on either side of the border, is the argument that even if feminist thinking influences the codification of a law, feminists are not likely to be the

---

1. The 1992 Pornography Victims' Compensation Act would have allowed victims of sexual crimes to bring suit against publishers, distributors, and retailers of pornography that triggered the violence against them. The Act failed to pass into law.

ones to enforce it. The situation in Canada could not have proved this better if it had been scripted. The first prosecution under Butler was of a lesbian-produced erotic magazine, *Bad Attitude*, seized from a gay and lesbian bookstore, Glad Day. When pro-sex feminists, gay activists, and civil libertarians demanded to know how woman-to-woman sex could fall afoul of a law that was meant to protect women from men, the convoluted answer indicated that the objectionable story (Trish Thomas's *"Wunna My Fantasies"*), because it depicted S/M sexual activity, *did* represent activity which was degrading to women—even though Thomas's narrative emphasized that the sex was happening in her head, not in real life! Exacerbating the defense's difficulties, Canada lacks a First Amendment.

Suppressing Access to Information

The feminists who seek to suppress pornography are quick to forget the history of obscenity legislation. Historically obscenity statutes have been used to suppress information important to women including contraception, abortion and sexually-transmitted disease information.

Edward H. Hurley, *Ethical Spectacle*, 1997.

The aftermath of Butler and the Glad Day trial was not pretty. Gay and lesbian shops received far more harassment under Butler than heterosexual porn stores. In particular Canada Customs targeted a small queer bookstore in Vancouver, BC, Little Sisters Book and Art Emporium. Little Sisters ultimately took Canada Customs to court for its practice of seizing books bound for the shop—this practice got so out of hand that Little Sisters's shelves were often nearly empty and even Dworkin's books were being held for suspicion of obscenity! Little Sisters won its case against Customs after several grueling years of legal battles, but they are aiming now to restrict Customs from targeting any other queer, women's or alternative bookstores. . . .

That teaming up with MacKinnon focused Dworkin's social theory into legal action is not surprising, since MacKinnon is an attorney. Nor is it surprising that their tactic involves redefining commonly-held understandings and legal definitions of words like obscenity and pornography. Mac-Kinnon's focus aside from and including her work with Dworkin is on words, language, and definitions—she is active in the fields of hate speech and sexual harassment law as well as pornography. The best-known and most focused anti-First Amendment attorney to come out of the feminist movement, MacKinnon has discovered a so-called progressive spin that justifies a position more often associated with the right wing. In her book *Only Words* she argues that speech itself can harm, and advocates restrictions on free speech to mitigate the damage done by racist and misogynist speech. Included in her definition of the latter, of course, is pornography. One notorious scene involving MacKinnon and her students at the University of Michigan involved them censoring a film festival featuring works by and about sex workers. This incident makes crystal clear one agenda of these women—they want to make sure that feminists who oppose them or offer contradictory information do not have a chance to speak up and be heard. To this end, they refuse to debate or appear on the same podium with pro-sex, anticensorship feminists. They appear to hope that their strategy—of providing the only accessible feminist position on sex—will be supported by the mainstream media, and in large part they have—so far—gotten their way.

Diana Russell

No other spokespersons for conservative feminism have received as much attention from the mainstream as MacKinnon and Dworkin. But within feminism, there are two more major figures who have contributed to the conservative feminist agenda. One is Diana Russell, sociology professor emerita (from Oakland's Mills College) and porn collector extraordinaire. Her most recent book, *Against Pornography: The Evidence of Harm* (1994) is larded with pornographic images, many of them extreme—or, as reviewer Jane Caputi, PhD, calls them, "standard women-hating, vicious and violent pornographic depictions." Typical of the conservative, anti-pornography feminist position is the redefinition of all or most pornography as violent. This is told to, and accepted as gospel by, those who have seen little or none, so that countless conservative feminists repeat this groundless assertion. Russell makes much of the fact that she reprinted images without the permission of the pornographers; she minimizes the fact that she is taking them out of context and often superimposing meanings that the original images were not produced to convey. This, too, is typical of anti-pornography demagogues.

Russell, aside from the time she has spent adding to her pornography collection, has been a tireless activist since the early days of the second wave feminist movement. She helped organize the First International Tribunal on Crimes Against Women, held in Brussels in 1976; she authored or edited books about rape, sexual exploitation, sex and violence, and S/M. The latter, *Against Sadomasochism* (1982), actually helped galvanize women in the S/M community to speak out against the S/M-bashing then so current within feminism. Most recently Russell has emerged to criticize the Milos Forman film, *The People Vs. Larry Flynt*.

Sex as a Problem

Kathleen Barry is also a sociology professor, whose main area of activism and influence has been anti-prostitution. Author in 1981 of *Female Sexual Slavery* (conservative feminism's favorite misnomer for prostitution) and in 1995 of *Prostitution of Sexuality: Global Exploitation of Women*, Barry is a nemesis of feminist sex work activists who favor decriminalization of prostitution and supportive services for prostitutes whether or not they desire to leave the sex industry. Predictably, Barry believes that engaging in prostitution cannot be a choice, and that it is always damaging and demeaning. She is very active on a global scale, consulting about prostitution and trafficking with United Nations Educational, Scientific and Cultural Organization (UNESCO). Last fall she was scheduled to appear at a conference about trafficking but canceled at the last minute, perhaps influenced in this decision by the news that two dozen members of the North American Task Force on Prostitution (a pro-feminist, pro-prostitution group) planned to attend.

As noted above, each of these women—and their supporters—tend to understand sexual speech and divergent sexual behaviors as problems, and they seek to leave no room for other women—even other feminists—to have different points of view about issues like pornography, prostitution, S/M, free speech, sexual harassment, male sexuality, etc. Though their points are expressed in feminist rhetoric and they have been and still are deeply dependent on feminism to give them a platform, they do not believe feminists ought to dialogue about or debate these issues. Indeed, when pro-sex feminists speak out, conservative feminists more often than not accuse them of not being feminists at all. At the same time they may network with anti-feminist conservatives to give themselves more clout.

Anti-Porn Feminists Hijack Feminism

What is to be done? Pro-sex feminists feel it's vital that other feminists, the media, and the mainstream hear that conservative feminist positions on sexual issues do not, by any means, represent all feminists. As many—or more—feminists are probably anti-censorship as pro-censorship, and many feminists are perfectly comfortable with the kind of sexual variations that conservative feminism decries as degrading to women. One can deeply believe in and work towards full equality for women and an end to misogynist abuse and harassment without jettisoning the First Amendment and women's right to express and explore their sexualities in a variety of ways, including for profit. Conservative feminists, like many other conservatives, regard free sexual expression and sexual exploration both with focused fascination and with great suspicion; they can neither turn away from nor accept hardcore images and sexual difference. Above all, while their concern for women's well-being is undoubtedly deep and genuine, they refuse to ask themselves why some women have negative experiences with porn, prostitution, and open sexuality while others do not. Beginning to answer this question might really help to make women's experiences with sex safer and better. But we need not look to conservative feminism for help, because their worldview disallows much female agency and flexibility and insists on seeing women as victims.

Every civil libertarian must speak out against the false

logic and information of the conservative feminists: as sex-positive feminist scholar and FACT co-founder Lisa Duggan notes (in her and Nan D. Hunter's book *Sex Wars: Sexual Dissent and Political Culture*), "This is political repression masked as a safety patrol, and it isn't Jesse Helms holding the stop sign." Other feminists' voices, though, are the most important of all, since within the shared understandings of feminism, we are best equipped to challenge this regressive ideology the media touts as representing the interests of women and those who love us. For the greatest damage done by the cult of conservative feminism may be the way it has sought to hijack feminism itself.

> "*Anti-pornography feminists believe that
> when violence and female subordination is
> presented as erotic, it encourages rape, wife
> abuse, incest, sexual harassment, femicide,
> and the view of women as non-persons.*"

Anti-Pornography Feminists Do Not Harm the Women's Movement

Ann E. Menasche

Ann E. Menasche is a feminist and civil rights lawyer. She argues in the following viewpoint that most of the efforts of anti-pornography feminists support the central objective of the women's movement: equal rights for women. She contends that all feminists should oppose pornography because it is hate speech that encourages sexual violence against women. Feminists who resort to name-calling and misrepresentation of the anti-pornography stance threaten to shut down the feminist debate about sexuality and pornography's effects on women, she argues.

As you read, consider the following questions:

1. According to Menasche, what is the main difference between the stances of anti-pornography feminists and those on the far-right who oppose pornography?
2. In the author's opinion, why have increasing numbers of women and girls turned to sex work?
3. How would the censorship of pornography harm the women's movement, according to Menasche?

Reprinted, with permission, from Ann E. Menasche, "Feminism and Pornography," *Against the Current*, June 26, 2000.

It was most unfortunate that Cathy Crosson in her review of Nadine Strossen's [president of the American Civil Liberties Union] book *Defending Pornography* chose to resort to anti-feminist stereotypes and name-calling to discredit anti-pornography activists with whom she disagrees. Such methods discourage real debate within the women's and progressive movements on a complex topic and, in a period of anti-feminist backlash, risk playing into the hands of the right wing far more than Dworkin-MacKinnon's mistaken approach to pornography.

Feminists Against Misogyny, Not Sex

The debate concerning what pornography is, and whether and how to oppose it has never been a question of being for or against "sex." Those who have read the primary sources with an open mind should be able to recognize that [feminists] like Andrea Dworkin, Catharine MacKinnon, Diana Russell and Kathleen Barry are no more "anti-sex" or "man-hating" than was Kate Millet, twenty-five years ago in her book *Sexual Politics*, exposing the misogyny in the sexual descriptions contained in Henry Miller's and D.H. Lawrence's novels. (Millet was called similar names at that time in an effort to discredit her.)

What Dworkin "et al." oppose is the same thing that Millet opposed in the heyday of the Second Wave [of the feminist movement], "the sexualized inequality of women." Says Dworkin:

> I see nothing to preclude that erotica could exist. . . . The fact of the matter is right now there is not an 'erotica' market. The pornography business is a $10 billion a year business and it is growing. . . . You couldn't sell didly-squat of anything that had to do with equality. . . . The way that you tell what pornography is, frankly, you look at the status of women in the material. Is it filled with hatred of women or isn't it? Does it use and violate women or doesn't it?

Pornography Is Hate Speech

Anti-pornography feminists see pornography as a form of hate speech, not unlike racist or anti-semitic propaganda or sexist advertising.

Unlike the right, none of the opponents of pornography

see sex and nudity itself as sinful, dirty or immoral. Neither do they hold traditional views of sexuality and gender roles; the exact opposite is the case. And none of them that I have read are biological essentialists about male violence, but neither do they deny its epidemic proportions in this society, as unfortunately Crosson seems to do.

Rather, anti-pornography feminists believe that when violence and female subordination is presented as erotic, it encourages rape, wife abuse, incest, sexual harassment, femicide, and the view of women as non-persons.

Crosson has confused the radical feminist critique of the heterosexual institution (particularly the compulsion, inequality, and violence within that institution under socially created—not biologically ordained—conditions of male supremacy), with Victorian attitudes against sex. These are simply not the same things, as any serious study of feminist writings over the last three decades would reveal. Taking quotes out of context, as Crosson does, does not prove otherwise.

Hate Speech Affects Hearts and Minds

One may disagree on how big an impact any particular form of hate speech has in encouraging bigotry and violence (Dworkin-MacKinnon seem to exaggerate the impact of pornography on women's status); however, it is hard to argue that such speech is completely harmless.

Speech (both the written and spoken word, pictures, etc.) does have the power to affect hearts and minds; otherwise, no one would ever bother writing anything. (If speech had no power, the putting out of the journal *Against the Current* would be a futile exercise.) A number of examples of the impact of hate speech come to mind: The fascistic book about race war and white supremacist "revolution," *The Turner Diaries*, probably helped inspire the Oklahoma City bombing.

Racist political ads aimed at immigrants from Mexico appear to contribute to violence against Latinos. Homophobia in the media or in campaign literature favoring anti-gay ballot initiatives can and does lead to gay-bashing. References to abortion as "murder" in anti-abortion publications or in the statements of the Catholic Church have most likely played a role in the recent murder of abortion doctors.

Pornography and Sexual Harassment

Certainly, presenting women and girls as mindless sexual objects who enjoy rape and violence might, in a similar fashion, encourage sexist violence. Moreover, if pornography were merely about "sex" and not about sexism, it is hard to imagine why pornography displayed at the workplace (pin-ups, etc.) has been held to be a form of sex discrimination against women workers.

That pornography is a particularly insidious form of sexist hate speech is illustrated by the fact that men who wish to force women out of the workplace utilize pornography, rather than, let's say, sexist advertising for laundry detergent. In truth, there are few things as effective as pornography to remind women of their "place."

The other problem with pornography pointed out by its opponents is that, unlike most other forms of hate speech, the production of pornography frequently involves the use of women and children in prostitution. Historically, neither socialists nor feminists have seen the selling of women's bodies as a free and liberating "choice" nor looked favorably upon pimps and capitalists that profit from this exploitation.

The pornography industry offers women some of the worst working conditions available, where sexual harassment is literally "part of the job." As the economy worsens and the social safety net is eliminated, more women and girls may be forced to turn to such "sex work" for their survival and the survival of their families.

Civil Remedies Against Pornography

In my opinion, the Dworkin-MacKinnon approach to fighting pornography is more problematic, but Crosson's misrepresentation of their views does nothing to enhance the debate. Dworkin and MacKinnon actually are opposed to all criminal obscenity laws. During the arguing of the Butler case in Canada,[1] Dworkin actively opposed the position of the Women's Legal Education and Action Fund, which urged the Canadian Supreme Court to reinterpret existing

1. In 1992, the Canadian Supreme Court expanded the legal definition of "obscenity" and made it illegal to import or distribute any printed or visual material that was "degrading" or "harmful" to women.

obscenity law in "sex equality" terms.

Dworkin-MacKinnon certainly had nothing to do with restrictions in the 1996 United States Communications Decency Act.[2] Instead, they advocate civil remedies against the pornography industry, including a cause of action for group defamation. The problem with this is that, in response to such private lawsuits for group defamation, courts would be empowered to issue injunctions against materials deemed pornographic.

Origins of the Anti-Pornography Movement

The real start of the feminist anti-pornography movement can probably be traced to a 1976 billboard in Los Angeles promoting the Rolling Stones. The billboard depicted a woman, tied up and bruised, with the caption: "I'm Black and Blue from the Rolling Stones—and I Love It!" Activists were similarly horrified two years later when *Hustler* ran a magazine cover depicting a woman being shoved into a meat grinder. The outrage these images engendered helped to fuel a variety of different feminist protests: the picketing of the magazines, tours of urban sex zones, and touring slide shows to graphically demonstrate the violence inherent in much of the pornography industry's product.

Frederick S. Lane III, *Obscene Profits: The Entrepreneurs of Pornography in the Cyber Age*, 2000.

Here I would agree with other civil libertarians that, in general, the danger of putting such power in the hands of the courts or other arm of the state in an attempt to suppress hate speech of any variety (whether racist, sexist, anti-semitic, or homophobic), outweighs the danger of allowing such speech to be published and limiting oneself to fighting against it in other ways.

Censorship Causes More Harm than Good

Crosson is correct that state censorship of pornography (as well as other hate speech) would backfire on the progressive movement and endanger positive sexual, artistic and politi-

---

2. The Communications Decency Act—which made it illegal to make indecent material accessible to minors on the Internet—was deemed unconstitutional by the U.S. Supreme Court in 1997.

cal expression. (Of course, there are situations in which speech becomes something else—sexual harassment, threats to personal safety, etc.—and can, in my view, be legitimately suppressed. There may also be privacy rights of individuals whose bodies are displayed in pornography and who no longer want this public exposure.)

It should be noted that other anti-pornography activists, such as Diana Russell, are for the suppression of both racist and sexist speech, showing a consistency that would hardly be the case if they were motivated by "Victorian" or "fundamentalist religious" impulses.

The Right-Wing Origins of Feminist-Bashing

Finally, Crosson is probably unaware of the right-wing origins of attempting to discredit feminists by calling them "manhaters" and accusing them of viewing women as "passive victims." Right-wing thinker Christine Hoff Sommers, in her anti-feminist diatribe "Who Stole Feminism?" accuses what she calls "gender feminists" of hating men and jeering at most American women:

> It is just not possible to incriminate men without implying that large numbers of women are fools or worse. . . . Since women today can no longer be regarded as the victims of an undemocratic indoctrination, we must regard their preferences as 'authentic.' Any other attitude toward American women is unacceptably patronizing and profoundly illiberal.

According to Summers, patriarchy or male domination is no longer a problem since women are already free. Likewise, in Naomi Wolf's profoundly conservative book *Fire with Fire: the New Female Power and How It Will Change the 21st Century*, Wolf proclaims that as of the 1992 election of Bill Clinton, women were at the brink of liberation, with only their bad self-images and a tendency to engage in "male-bashing" getting in the way of final victory.

Wolf posits two types of feminism: "victim feminism" which is "anti-sex," "anti-male" and portrays women as helpless victims, and "power feminism" which embraces women's "power" and "success" in the capitalist world. Like Crosson, Wolf states that "victim feminism" has turned off most women who can't relate to its negativity toward men and (hetero)sexuality.

Needed: A Respectful Exchange

By pointing out these connections, I do not mean to imply that Crosson herself is right wing, or to cast doubt on the sincerity of her feminist and socialist views. Rather, I hope to convince her (and others who agree with her) to reconsider the advisability of engaging in such methods of debate with other feminists and of dismissing outright the radical feminist contribution to understanding sexuality. Socialists have a lot to learn from radical feminists; it is simply not a one-way street.

From a more even-handed and respectful exchange, a more enlightened socialist-feminism might emerge: one that would take seriously all the ways women have been denied equal dignity and personhood in this society, not merely the economic aspects of female oppression, but the ideological, interpersonal and sexual aspects as well; that would not apologize for or minimize the problems of male sexism and violence, any more than we would deny the dangers posed by white racism or accuse those who expose the persistence of racist violence and discrimination of creating an "ethos of victimhood;" a socialist-feminism that would recognize that by women naming our oppression, we are not engaging in "victimtalk" or "hating men" but creating the basis of a movement for change; and that presents a vision of socialism where male domination, sexual violence and abuse—"the eroticization of women's subordination"—would be a thing of the past.

In struggling to achieve such a vision, we may be called upon to defend pornography on free speech grounds, but we would never glorify it.

Periodical Bibliography

The following articles have been selected to supplement the diverse views presented in this chapter. Addresses are provided for periodicals not indexed in the *Readers' Guide to Periodical Literature*, the *Alternative Press Index*, the *Social Sciences Index*, or the *Index to Legal Periodicals and Books*.

Amy Allen	"Rethinking Power," *Hypatia*, January 1, 1998.
Andrea Dworkin	"The Day I Was Drugged and Raped," *New Statesman*, June 5, 2000.
Joanne Furio	"Does Women's Equality Depend on What We Do About Pornography?" *Ms.*, January/February 1995.
Wendy McElroy	"A Feminist Defense of Pornography," *Free Inquiry*, Fall 1997. Available from PO Box 664, Amherst, NY 14226-0664.
Wendy McElroy	"Whores vs. Feminists," *Liberty*, January 1999. Available from 1018 Water St., Suite 201, Port Townsend, WA 98368.
Ann E. Menasche	"An Interview with Diana Russell: Violence, Pornography, and Woman-Hating," *Against the Current*, July/August 1997.
Dennis Prager	"Divinity and Pornography," *Weekly Standard*, June 14, 1999. Available from 1211 Avenue of the Americas, New York, NY 10036.
Diana E.H. Russell	"Nadine Strossen: The Pornography Industry's Wet Dream," *On the Issues*, Summer 1995.
Nadine Strossen	"Big Sister Is Watching You," *Advocate*, November 14, 1995.
Nadine Strossen	"The Perils of Pornophobia," *Humanist*, May/June 1995.

For Further Discussion

Chapter 1

1. Lisa Palac—who works in the pornography industry—argues that pornography is not harmful to individuals and society. In your opinion, do Hall's personal experiences with pornography strengthen or weaken her argument? Explain.

2. The National Coalition for the Protection of Children and Families argues that obscenity harms society. In your opinion, does the legal definition of obscenity make clear the difference between "hard-core" pornography which is not protected by the First Amendment and other pornography which is protected? Point to specific wording in the legal definition to support your argument.

3. Julia Wilkins claims that the media exaggerate the extent of Internet pornography in order to sell magazines and newspapers. On the other hand, Mark Laaser draws on his own experience with pornography to argue that cyberporn is a serious problem. In your opinion, what are the advantages and disadvantages of relying on primary sources—which include personal testimonies like Laaser's—to form opinions about controversial issues? What are the advantages and disadvantages of relying on secondary sources—which include most magazine and newspaper articles?

4. Diana E.H. Russell supports her argument that pornography causes violence by citing various studies. Conversely, Mathew Gever points to historical records to support his position that pornography does not cause violence against women. Examine the evidence that each writer uses and discuss its strengths and weaknesses. In your opinion, which author makes the more convincing argument? Why?

Chapter 2

1. James K. Fitzpatrick argues that pornography should be censored in order to create shame in those who view it illegally. Do you believe that public disapproval of controversial beliefs or practices eradicates those beliefs or practices? Cite concrete examples to support your argument.

2. Avedon Carol maintains that pornography should be made accessible so that people can form their own opinions about it. The United States, however, has many laws that limit what people have access to, including obscenity laws that limit what kinds of

pornography people will see and laws limiting what drugs people can ingest. Do you think such laws unnecessarily infringe on people's freedom, or do they protect the common good? Explain your answer using specific laws to illustrate your points.

3. John P. Araujo claims that pornography belittles women. Wendy McElroy disagrees, arguing that it is governments that dictate what women can do with their bodies, and radical feminists—claiming women cannot make adult decisions—who belittle women. Can laws—such as obscenity laws that censor pornography—succeed in changing people's minds about social issues such as the worth of women?

4. The Center for Reclaiming America asserts that artistic merit should be judged according to the standards of decency held by the majority. Conversely, Robert Brustein claims that judging works of art according to the majority's sense of decency silences the minority opinions necessary for democracy. Do you think majority opinions are superior to minority opinions? Why or why not? Support your answer with examples from history and/or your experience.

Chapter 3

1. Maryam Kubasek contends that the government should protect children from pornography on the Internet by censoring online obscenity. Stephen Chapman maintains that adult supervision—not censorship, which he claims is unconstitutional—would protect children from Internet pornography just as it always has. In what ways are traditional venues that offer pornography—such as bookstores, convenience stores, and video stores—different from an electronic medium such as the Internet? Do those differences support Kubasek's argument for censorship or Chapman's argument against it? Explain your answer.

2. Solveig Bernstein supports the use of filtering software to protect children from Internet pornography. However, Langdon Winner claims that such software also blocks out non-pornographic websites of which the software manufacturer disapproves. Which do you think would harm children more, viewing hardcore pornography on the Internet or having their Internet searches restricted by someone else's political agenda? Explain your answer.

3. Mark Y. Herring maintains that libraries should install filtering software on their computers in order to protect children from Internet pornography. Charles Levendosky asserts that such regulation would limit what adults could view, a restriction that would infringe on their constitutional rights. In your opinion, is it more

important to protect children from pornography or to protect the rights of adults to have access to unrestricted information?

Chapter 4

1. John Stoltenberg argues that feminists should continue to oppose pornography because it harms women. However, Lynne Segal argues that feminists should focus instead on changing the cultural institutions that oppress women because pornography is merely a symptom of that oppression. In your opinion, can the effort people make to effect minor changes in their lives or their world lead to more significant changes? In other words, do you believe that opposing pornography might eventually help re-shape people's attitudes and the institutions that serve them? Please explain.

2. Carol Queen maintains that anti-pornography feminists hurt the women's movement by silencing other feminists who do not agree that pornography harms women. In particular, she argues that Andrea Dworkin and Catharine MacKinnon refuse to engage in dialogue about pornography's harmful effects on women. Do you think it is ever beneficial to refuse to debate a controversial issue such as pornography? Explain your answer.

3. Ann E. Menasche asserts that critics of anti-pornography feminism often hurt the women's movement by misrepresenting the arguments of other feminists. In your opinion, would Ann E. Menasche consider Carol Queen's article a misrepresentation of the anti-pornography stance? Cite specific sections of both authors' texts to formulate your argument.

Organizations to Contact

The editors have compiled the following list of organizations concerned with the issues debated in this book. The descriptions are derived from materials provided by the organizations. All have publications or information available for interested readers. The list was compiled on the date of publication of the present volume; the information provided here may change. Be aware that many organizations take several weeks or longer to respond to inquiries, so allow as much time as possible.

Adult Video Association
270 N. Canon Dr., Suite 1370, Beverly Hills, CA 90210
(213) 650-7121

The association believes adults should be able to watch what they choose in the privacy of their own homes. It challenges the constitutionality of laws affecting adult videos. The association provides legal information and referrals, lobbies government agencies, maintains a speakers bureau, and conducts educational programs. It publishes a periodic newsletter.

American Civil Liberties Union (ACLU)
132 W. 43rd St., New York, NY 10036
(212) 944-9800 • fax: (212) 869-9065
website: www.aclu.org

The ACLU champions the human rights set forth in the U.S. Constitution. It works to protect the rights of all Americans and to promote equality for women, minorities, and the poor. The ACLU opposes censorship and believes that other measures should be used to combat the harms of pornography. The organization publishes a variety of handbooks, pamphlets, reports, and newsletters, including the quarterly *Civil Liberties* and the monthly *Civil Liberties Alert*.

Canadian Civil Liberties Association
229 Yonge St., Suite 403, Toronto, ON M5B 1N9 Canada
(416) 363-0321 • fax: (416) 861-1291
e-mail: ccla@ilap.com • website: www.ccla.org

The association works to protect Canadians' civil liberties and to educate the public concerning civil liberties. It opposes censorship of pornography. Among the association's many publications are the books *When Freedoms Collide: The Case for Our Civil Liberties and Uncivil Obedience* and the monthly *CCLA News Notes*.

Citizens Against Pornography (CAP)
1016 N. 560 W., Suite #1, Logan, UT 84341
(801) 355-8368
e-mail: stoporn@yahoo.com
CAP fights the proliferation and sale of magazines such as *Penthouse* and *Playboy* at retail outlets. It also seeks to stop the production and distribution of adult videos and the opening of adult bookstores. CAP provides information to anyone interested in combating pornography.

Citizens for Media Responsibility Without Law
PO Box 2085, Rancho Cordova, CA 95741-2085
(408) 427-2858
Citizens for Media Responsibility Without Law opposes violent pornography. Rather than advocating censorship, however, it believes that the media should take responsibility for not producing or selling violent images. The organization also encourages civil disobedience as an effective way to stop the proliferation of pornography without resorting to censorship. It publishes leaflets and position papers.

Concerned Women for America (CWA)
1015 Fifteenth St. NW, Suite 1100, Washington, DC 20005
(202) 488-7000 • fax: (202) 488-0806
e-mail: mail@cwfa.org • website: www.cwfa.org
CWA's purpose is to preserve, protect, and promote traditional Judeo-Christian values through education, legislative action, and other activities. It believes that pornography harms all of society and should be censored. CWA publishes the monthly *Family Voice* in addition to brochures, booklets, and manuals on numerous issues, including pornography.

Family Research Council
801 G St. NW, Washington, DC 20001
(202) 393-2100 • fax: (202) 393-2134
e-mail: corrdept@frc.org • website: www.frc.org
The council seeks to promote and protect the interests of the traditional family. It opposes pornography as harmful to children and families. The council publishes the monthly newsletter *Washington Watch* in addition to policy papers on a variety of political and social issues.

Feminists Against Censorship (FAC)

BM Box 207, London, England WC1N 3XX
e-mail: avedon@cix.compulink.co.uk
website: www.fiawol/demon.co.uk/FAC

FAC works to fight censorship from a feminist perspective. FAC believes that censoring pornography harms women's rights.

Feminists Fighting Pornography

Box 6731, Yorkville Station, New York, NY 10128
(212) 410-5182

Feminists Fighting Pornography lobbies Congress to pass laws regulating pornography. It maintains a speakers bureau and conducts audiovisual presentations. The organization publishes the annual magazine *Backlash Times.*

Feminists for Free Expression (FFE)

2525 Times Square, New York, NY 10108
e-mail: FFE@aol.com • website: www.well.com/user/freedom

FFE works to preserve the women's right and responsibility to read, listen, view, and produce materials of her choice, without intervention of the state for "her own good." FFE believes that freedom of expression is especially important for women's rights. The organization publishes materials on pornography and censorship such as the pamphlet, "Pornography."

Free Speech Coalition

22968 Victory Blvd., Suite 248, Woodland Hills, CA 91367
(818) 348-9373

The coalition is the trade association of the adult entertainment and products industry. Members of the coalition believe censoring pornography violates the right of Americans to free speech. The coalition publishes pro-pornography, anti-censorship materials and a sourcebook on the pornography prosecutions and laws throughout the United States.

Men Against Pornography

PO Box 150786, Brooklyn, NY 11215-0786
e-mail: map-usa@geocities.com
website: www.geocities.com/CapitolHill/1139/Index.html

Men Against Pornography is a national feminist organization that works to reduce the harm caused by pornography. The organization's website provides a forum for men who are recovering from pornography addiction to share their stories with others. The organization also disseminates information about pornography's effects on women.

Morality in Media (MIM)
475 Riverside Dr., Suite 239, New York, NY 10115
(212) 870-3222 • fax: (212) 870-2765
e-mail: mim@moralityinmedia.org
website: www.moralityinmedia.org

MIM is a national, interfaith organization working to stop illegal trafficking in hardcore pornography through the rigorous enforcement of state and federal obscenity laws. It works to alert and inform the public and government officials about the destructive effects of pornography. MIM has a National Obscenity Law Center, which is a clearinghouse of legal information on obscenity cases. While the group opposes censorship, it believes that obscenity laws should be strictly enforced and that hardcore pornography is not a protected form of speech. It publishes a bimonthly newsletter in addition to educational materials such as *Pornography Has Consequences* and the handbook *TV: The World's Greatest Mind-Bender.*

National Campaign for Freedom of Expression
1429 G St. NW, PMB #416, Washington, DC 20005-2009
(202) 393-2787
e-mail: ncfe@ncfe.net • website: www.ncfe.net

The National Campaign for Freedom of Expression is a group of artists, art organizations, and other individuals concerned with fighting censorship of the visual and performance arts. It believes that individuals have a right to determine for themselves what they want to see. The organization offers technical assistance and training to local activists, monitors legislation, provides legal assistance, distributes press releases, conducts educational programs, and maintains a speakers bureau. Its library contains reference clippings and periodicals, and it publishes the quarterly *NCFE Bulletin* and a newsletter.

National Coalition Against Censorship (NCAC)
275 Seventh Ave., New York, NY 10001
(212) 807-NCAC • fax: (212) 807-6245
website: www.ncac.org

NCAC's goal is to fight censorship, including the censorship of pornography. It fights censorship through conferences, educational programs, and community activism. The coalition publishes the newsletter *Censorship News* and educational materials such as *The Sex Panic: Women, Censorship, and Pornography.*

National Coalition for the Protection of Children & Families
800 Compton Rd., Suite 9224, Cincinnati, OH 45231-9964
(513) 521-6227 • fax: (513) 521-6337
e-mail: ncpcf@eos.net • website: www.nationalcoalition.org

The coalition, formerly called the National Coalition Against Pornography, was formed in 1983 to help stop the harm caused by obscenity and child pornography. It is an alliance of citizens and civic, business, religious, health care, and educational groups working to eliminate child pornography and to remove illegal pornography from the marketplace. The coalition lobbies legislatures and educates the public and law enforcement officials on the dangers of pornography. Its National Law Center for Children and Families is a clearinghouse for legal information on child exploitation and illegal pornography. The coalition publishes brochures such as *Children, Pornography, and Cyberspace*.

National Federation for Decency
PO Drawer 2440, Tupelo, MS 38803
(601) 844-5036

The federation works to improve the morality of America. It opposes pornography and advocates the censorship of all pornographic materials. The federation sponsors decency campaigns and publishes a newsletter.

Women Against Pornography
PO Box 845, Times Square Post Office, New York, NY 10108-0845
(212) 307-5055

Women Against Pornography is a national organization that educates the public about the harm pornography does to the safety and status of all women. It conducts tours of New York City's Times Square to demonstrate that pornography is readily available. Women Against Pornography works with other organizations to lobby legislatures to censor pornography and publishes educational information on the harms of pornography.

Women's Action Alliance
370 Lexington Ave., Suite 603, New York, NY 10017
(212) 532-8330 • fax: (212) 779-2846

The alliance was established in 1971 as a national nonprofit service organization that provides educational services and programs to help women become self-sufficient and independent. It publishes educational materials on pornography and *Women in Action*, a quarterly newsletter.

Bibliography of Books

Robert M. Baird and Stuart A. Rosenbaum — *Pornography: Private Right or Public Menace?* Buffalo: Prometheus Books, 1998.

Avedon Carol — *Nudes, Prudes, and Attitudes: Pornography and Censorship*. Cheltenham, UK: New Clarion Press, 1994.

Fred H. Cate — *Internet and the First Amendment: Schools and Sexually Explicit Expression*. Bloomington, IN: Phi Delta Kappa, 1998.

Drucilla Cornell, ed. — *Feminism and Pornography*. Oxford: Oxford University Press, 2000.

Barry M. Dank and Roberto Refinetti, eds. — *Sex Work and Sex Workers*. New Brunswick: Transaction Publishers, 1999.

Frederique Delacoste, ed. — *Sex Work: Writings by Women in the Sex Industry*. New York: Cleis Press, 1998.

Andrea Dworkin — *Intercourse*. New York: Free Press, 1997.

Andrea Dworkin — *Life and Death: Unapologetic Writings on the Continuing War Against Women*. New York: Free Press, 1997.

Andrea Dworkin — *Pornography: Men Possessing Women*. New York: Dutton, 1991.

James Elias et al. — *Porn 101: Eroticism, Pornography, and the First Amendment*. Buffalo: Prometheus Books, 1999.

Owen M. Fiss — *The Irony of Free Speech*. Cambridge, MA: Harvard University Press, 1996.

Susan Gubar and Joan Hoff, eds. — *For Adult Users Only: The Dilemma of Violent Pornography*. Bloomington: Indiana University Press, 1989.

Rochelle Gurstein — *The Repeal of Reticence: A History of America's Cultural and Legal Struggles over Free Speech, Obscenity, Sexual Liberation, and Modern Art*. New York: Hill and Wang, 1998.

Laurie Hall — *An Affair of the Mind: One Woman's Courageous Battle to Salvage Her Family from the Devastation of Pornography*. Colorado Springs, CO: Focus on the Family, 1996.

Maureen Harrison and Steve Gilbert, eds. — *Obscenity and Pornography: Decisions of the United States Supreme Court*. New York: Excellent Books, 2000.

Donna Rice Hughes — *Kids Online: Protecting Your Children in Cyberspace*. New York: Fleming H. Revell, 1998.

June Juffer	*At Home with Pornography: Women, Sex, and Everyday Life*. New York: New York University Press, 1998.
Walter Kendrick	*The Secret Museum: Pornography in Modern Culture*. Berkeley: University of California Press, 1996.
Michael S. Kimmell, ed.	*Men Confront Pornography*. New York: Meridian, 1990.
Laurie Kipnis	*Bound and Gagged: Pornography and the Politics of Fantasy in America*. New York: Grove Press, 1996.
Frederick S. Lane	*Obscene Profits: The Entrepreneurs of Pornography in the Cyber Age*. New York: Routledge, 2000.
Catharine MacKinnon	*Only Words*. Cambridge, MA: Harvard University Press, 1993.
Catharine MacKinnon and Andrea Dworkin	*In Harm's Way: The Pornography Civil Rights Hearings*. Cambridge, MA: Harvard University Press, 1998.
Wendy McElroy	*XXX: A Woman's Right to Pornography*. New York: St. Martin's Press, 1995.
Lisa Palac	*The Edge of the Bed: How Dirty Pictures Changed My Life*. Boston, MA: Little, Brown, 1998.
Martin Rimm	*Pornographer's Handbook: How to Exploit Women, Dupe Men, and Make Lots of Money*. Pittsburgh: Carnegie Mellon University Press, 1995.
Diana E.H. Russell	*Dangerous Relationships: Pornography, Misogyny, and Rape*. Thousand Oaks, CA: Sage Publications, 1998.
John Stoltenberg	*Refusing to Be a Man: Essays on Sex and Justice*. New York: UCL Press, 2000.
John Stoltenberg	*What Makes Pornography "Sexy"?* Minneapolis: Milkweed Editions, 1994.
Nadine Strossen	*Defending Pornography: Free Speech, Sex, and the Fight for Women's Rights*. New York: New York University Press, 2001.
Yaron Svoray	*Gods of Death*. New York: Simon and Schuster, 1997.
U.S. Attorney General's Commission on Pornography	*Final Report of the Attorney General's Commission on Pornography*. Nashville: Rutledge Hill Press, 1986.
James Weinstein	*Hate Speech, Pornography, and the Radical Attack on Free Speech*. New York: Westview Press, 1999.
Ronald Weitzer, ed.	*Sex for Sale: Prostitution, Pornography, and the Sex Industry*. New York: Routledge, 2000.

Index